Ensamble Studio

 Published under license from Editorial Gustavo Gili. *2G* was founded in 1997 as an international architecture magazine by Editorial Gustavo Gili, evolving, over the years, into a monographic magazine and international reference. Since 2016 it is published under license by Koenig Books.

Director and editor Moisés Puente

Graphic design RafamateoStudio

Translation and proofreading George Hutton

Cover photograph Iwan Baan

Lithography Rovira Digital, Barcelona

Print agpograf impressors, Barcelona

First published by Verlag der Buchhandlung Walther und Franz König, Cologne

Verlag der Buchhandlung Walther und Franz König
Ehrenstrasse 4
D-50672 Köln
verlag@buchhandlung-walther-koenig.de

Printed in Spain
ISBN: 978-3-96098-806-9

Distribution

Germany, Austria and Switzerland
Buchhandlung Walther König, Cologne
Tel. +49 (0) 221 / 20 59 6-53
Fax +49 (0) 221 / 20 59 6-60
verlag@buchhandlung-walther-koenig.de

Distribution outside the United States and Canada, Germany, Austria and Switzerland
Thames & Hudson Ltd., London
www.thamesandhudson.com

United States and Canada
D.A.P. / Distributed Art Publishers, Inc., New York
www.artbook.com

MIX
Paper from responsible sources
FSC® C104592

Contents

Like the seas and oceans that ebb and flow, following the gravitation of the Moon, architecture also seems to be affected by tidal forces. For most of the 20th century, these forces appeared to be drawing buildings away from the Earth. It was as if they needed to be anchored to the ground to stop them from floating away, from dissolving and melting into the air. During the heyday of the industrialised societies, when fossil fuel was virtually free and the carbon trapped underground could not be released into the atmosphere fast enough, buildings and cities were triumphing over the laws of nature. More recently, though, the gravitational forces have changed. The age of weightlessness is over. Nowadays, buildings and cities are drawn downwards, towards the terrain, even into the ground. They appear to merge with the earth; they mimic its texture and colour. Today, the glass and steel skyscrapers look anachronistic, like dreams from another era.

Philip Ursprung is Professor of the History of Art and Architecture at the Department of Architecture at ETH Zurich. From 2017 to 2019 he was Dean of the Department. He is editor of *Herzog & de Meuron: Natural History* (Montreal, 2002) and author of *Allan Kaprow, Robert Smithson, and the Limits to Art* (Berkeley, 2013). His most recent books are *Brechas y conexiones. Ensayos sobre arquitectura, arte y economía* (Barcelona, 2016), *Der Wert der Oberfläche* (Zurich, 2017), and *Representation of Labor/Performative Historiography* (Santiago, 2018).

Architecture and Anthropocene

Since the turn of the Millennium, the trend towards the ground, towards the earth, its soil, minerals, and depth, has a name—the Anthropocene. The concept of the Anthropocene, a geological age induced by humans, or, more precisely, by those human societies that brought about industrialisation, is the horizon for current politics and discourses. The Anthropocene is intrinsically linked to the notion of climate change and global warming. The discussion thereof shakes up our long-established understandings of time, traditional hierarchies and categories.

To some extent, the notion of the Anthropocene has replaced the notion of nature. It has become difficult to speak of nature without quotation marks—in other words, it is hard not to regard nature as a cultural concept that can be historicised, as a fiction, so to speak. Within the horizon of the Anthropocene, nature can no longer be considered as an opposition to culture. This old dichotomy gives way to new ideas of interdependency and ecosystems. As a result, the traditional hierarchy of the living and the non-living, of the human and the non-human, is called into question. Human time is considered in its relation to geological time. Glaciers "die" in front of one's eyes. Viruses, which are neither dead nor alive, affect the lives of animals and humans. The spate of droughts in the Middle East was one of the causes of the Syrian civil war and the subsequent refugee crisis. Even some volcanic eruptions are partially induced by a change in pressure of the Earth's crust, following the melting of the polar ice caps. In the perspective of the Anthropocene, the Earth is not an eternal reservoir of resources and time—instead, it is at the mercy of the pressure caused by industrialised societies. As such, the Earth is not a realm of eternity, but rather it is subject to urgency.

There are many definitions of the Anthropocene. Scholars debate whether it starts with early humans building a fire, with the dawn of industrialisation, or with the atomic bomb. Precisely because this concept is not strictly defined, it serves as a lively meeting point for discussing the crossover of topics that had otherwise seemed unrelated. Whereas the notion of globalisation is driven by the centres of the capitalist world, and is perceived from the perspective of power, the notion of the Anthropocene brings to light the perspectives of the powerless, the colonised, those who suffer from the dark side of industrialisation. In this regard, Elizabeth Povinelli coined the concept of "geontology" in her book *Geontologies: A Requiem to Late Liberalism.*[1] By "geontology" she understands the ontology, or being, of something geological that is not alive but that is intrinsically connected to what is alive. For Povinelli, "the emergence of the geological concept of the Anthropocene and the meteorological modelling of the carbon cycle [...] point to the perforating boundary between the autonomy of Life and its opposition to a difference from Nonlife".[2]

1 — Povinelli, Elizabeth, *Geontologies: A Requiem to Late Liberalism*, Durham: Duke University Press, 2016.

2 — *Ibid.*, p. 14.

Whereas the arts and the humanities are keen to make their voices heard in the debate around the Anthropocene, architecture has, thus far, mostly remained silent.[3] The architectural work of Ensamble Studio is well suited to discuss the question of architecture within the current debate. This does not imply that Ensamble Studio illustrates the concept of the Anthropocene, and nor does it mean that their central aim is to develop technologies and materials that reduce carbon emissions or energy consumption. Rather, they combine the technological and the aesthetic approach. With their WoHo projects, they conduct research into certain offsite technologies and housing typologies which seek to solve problems and optimise the construction process. At the same time, they design spaces that heighten awareness about our relationship with the environment. The architecture of Ensamble Studio works like a sensor that allows us to perceive the current change more clearly, and as a proposal for improving architecture and fabrication, for a more sustainable building industry.

One of their leitmotivs, so to speak, is gravity. This is apparent in numerous buildings: the Hemeroscopium House, which is assembled from gigantic concrete beams; the Zig Zag House project, which appears to slide down a slope towards a lake; or the Telcel Theatre in the heart of Mexico City, which draws the spectators down, like into a crater. They are all particularly sensitive to the forces that pull down, towards the earth. The other leitmotiv is the mediation between the human and non-human scales. Their investigation of this theme starts with the cyclopean granite walls of the Musical Studies Centre in Santiago de Compostela, Spain, then the SGAE Headquarters, also in Santiago de Compostela, made out of huge granite boulders, followed by the concrete slabs inserted into the former factory space for the Reader's House in Madrid. The architecture of Ensamble Studio articulates forces and tensions, making them visible and tangible. In short, it gives a face to the abstract notion of the Anthropocene, and it contributes to an aesthetic of the Anthropocene.

Concrete folly

The 6-minute video *The Truffle* (2010), by Ensamble Studio, starts with a shot of a concrete nozzle, descending from the sky.[4] The nozzle comes down slowly, getting closer and closer to the camera, until the screen is all black. The construction machine is filmed from the ground. We see it from the perspective of the earth, as it were, which anxiously awaits the moment when the concrete mass starts to pour.

Cut. The camera changes position. It records the production process in a time-lapse. Workers pour layer after layer of concrete into a clearing in the ground. Hay bales are placed in the centre to make up the core, protected by plastic sheets. A bulldozer brings in more earth that serves as formwork. The final layer is covered

3 — Helene Romakin is researching this issue, on a broader scale, as part of her dissertation "The Anthropocene and Visual Culture". I am grateful for her discussion, which brought this issue to my attention.

4 — *The Truffle*, A Franchetau Film, video, 6 min., 2010.

Musical Studies Centre, Santiago de Compostela, Spain, 2002.
© Iwan Baan

with soil. Once the concrete has hardened, the earth is removed, and the result is an artificial boulder. Its irregular and messy surface is an imprint of the earth. In the words of the architects, "the land provided the concrete with its texture and colour, its form and its essence, and concrete gave the earth its strength and internal structure".[5] It resembles a foundling, left behind by a retreating glacier. Or a meteorite that has crashed onto Earth. Or a gigantic truffle, dug out from the roots of a tree. The workers come back and cut up the shell with a concrete saw. The soft core, made of hay, is revealed, just like the fudgy centre of a gigantic chocolate truffle.

Cut. The camera points skywards again. Suddenly, the head of a calf appears. We see the hay from the animal's perspective. It starts eating the hay, hollowing out the space inside the concrete mass. By the end of the summer, it has grown into a cow—it now weighs 300 kg, having consumed all the hay. It created an interior space. Workers come back to attach a door, a window, and a chimney on the outside. A bed, a toilet and a fireplace are installed within the structure. The space is now ready for humans to inhabit.

What exactly is The Truffle? A holiday guesthouse, overlooking the Costa da Morte (the 'Death Coast') in northern Spain? A hermit's hideaway, for someone to escape the busy city for a while, and enjoy some solitude amid the seemingly untouched landscape? A cave, sheltering its inhabitants? Many associations spring to mind, from Claude-Nicolas Ledoux's utopian project for the House of the Farm Guards, to Henri David Thoreau's hut near Walden Pond, Le Corbusier's Cabanon, and Absalon's *Cellules*.

As an object, The Truffle has all the qualities of a folly, an architectural genre that has almost died out today. Follies were popular in landscape architecture from the 16th to the early 19th century. They are to architecture what concepts are to lan-

5 — Ensamble Studio, "The Truffle", statement, undated, n.p.

guage and experiments to science, i.e. set-ups where new ideas are tried out, and where meaning is negotiated. Some follies have no function at all, such as fake ruins. Others resemble temples, or hermit grottoes. They often mimic real buildings, natural formations or even fruit, such as the Dunmore Pineapple in Scotland. Located somewhere between sculpture and architecture, between utility and decoration, between reality and imagination, a folly is an opportunity to raise questions.

The Truffle touches upon a series of issues. On the one hand, it is about the joy of creation. The builders clearly take great pleasure in digging, pouring, and moving matter, and they enjoy being surprised by the results. It is about a form taking shape, emerging from a formless mass. It is about the minimum requirements of a house: in The Truffle, one can sleep, build a fire, cook, use the toilet. There is a door, a window, and a chimney. Of course, practicality is not the main aim of The Truffle. It is also a built manifesto.

In the video showing the process behind The Truffle, we see how production and consumption are blended together, as well as work and leisure. It would be easy to dismiss The Truffle as an unnecessary luxury. Just like the chocolate ones, or the expensive mushroom, there is no pressing need for such a building. However, it allows one to take new, unanticipated perspectives. Not merely the perspective of the inhabitant who overlooks the cliffs, but also the perspective of the dead matter, the soil which is to be covered in concrete. Eventually, it also allows one to take the perspective of the calf, the animal that eats up the hay. As Gordon Matta-Clark put it, half a century ago, "cows live in eatable space but architects don't".[6]

Earth Pavilions

Ensamble Studio continue this line of experimentation that started with The Truffle, and they scale it up for their Structures of Landscape at the Tippet Rise Art Center in Fishtail, Montana. This art hub, located in a ranch north of Yellowstone Park, combines outdoor sculptures, musical performances and architectural spaces. Visitors can enjoy a synaesthetic experience of music, artificial spaces and the landscape. If The Truffle can be defined as a folly, the three structures here, namely the Beartooth Portal, the Inverted Portal and the Domo, as well as the planned Tabula Acustica, can be defined as pavilions. They look like spontaneous constructions, like tents set up in the land. They provide shelter from the wind, rain and snow, but they remain open to the elements; they have no doors or windows, and no heating.

They address the difference between what is manmade and what is formed by nature. As with The Truffle, the shape of these structures is achieved by pouring concrete into clearings in the earth. The concrete structure takes on the shape and texture of the hole in the ground, reflecting its matter. The Portals consist of two

6 — Matta-Clark, Gordon, "The Nature of Occupation", manuscript text, undated, in Moure, Gloria (ed.), *Gordon Matta-Clark*, Madrid: Museo Nacional Centro de Arte Reina Sofía, 2006, p. 363.

separate slabs leaning against each other, as if balanced there by a childish giant, messing around with pebbles. The Domo is a monolithic mass, reminiscent of a prehistoric stone grave or an archaic temple.

The purpose of the Domo is to host musical performances. It overcomes the traditional separation between the performer and the audience and the environment. It defines, or marks, a space of the visible and the audible. Like the sounds that emerge from the human body interacting with cords, membranes, metal, expanding through the air, bouncing off the floor or the ceiling and entering the human ear, the surfaces of the concrete pillars and roof contain imprints of the structure of the earth. The way the sound touches the ear is echoed in the imprinting of one matter into another matter. There is a continuous resonance between instruments, concrete, human bodies and the surrounding landscape. In a way, the pavilion is a huge instrument in itself.

The structures in the land evoke the spectacular works of Earth Art from the 1970s, such as Robert Smithson's *Spiral Jetty*, Michael Heizer's *Double Negative*, and Nancy Holt's *Sun Tunnels*. These interventions, far removed from any gallery or museum walls, use the land as a backdrop to the art, and the art as a frame for perceiving the land. They are characteristic of a period when the boundaries between art and architecture were more open, when the hierarchies of the genres were unfixed. They bear witness to an early phase of environmental consciousness and the caring for the Earth as a whole—think of "Earth Day", first celebrated in 1970—which pre-empt the notion of the Anthropocene.

Despite the formal proximity between these canonical artworks, built half a century ago, and the architecture of Ensamble Studio, there are also substantial differences. Earth Art is emblematic of the expansion of art, and the art world, in the late 20th century. The works by Smithson, Heizer, Holt and other artists of the genre are rooted in sculpture. The production of these artworks in remote areas of the American West, around the same time as the moon landing, symbolises the prevailing ideology of progress, innovation, and growth in the 1970s. The pavilions by Ensamble Studio, however, depart from architecture. And instead of an ideology of progress, they pursue the idea of going back in time, to archaic shapes and building methods. The techniques used are rudimentary—bulldozers, cranes, shovels—and no energy is needed to maintain the structures once in place.

Underground Utopia

The research into the relationship between architecture and geology, between living beings and dead matter, air and solid material, all of which is in play in both The Truffle and the structures at the Tippet Rise Art Center, is further developed in the Ca'n Terra on the island of Menorca. The architects gradually carve a home into a former stone quarry, which was also temporarily used for military purposes before being abandoned. In this project, the process of colonising space, of occupying the ground, of destruction, which is unavoidable when building, is reduced to a minimum. The only operation that actually destroys an existing structure, namely the cutting out of a piece of the ground, in fact brings light into the dark.

Again, the project video clearly sets out the architects' intentions. The cut-out rock is covered by soil and a small tree. When this piece crashes to the ground, the tree remains there, standing firm amid the light pouring in from the ceiling, like a decorative plant.

Ca'n Terra is a network of caverns. It recalls antique catacombs, or the cave structure of Naples, i.e. the former quarries in the volcanic stone that served as religious spaces, burial grounds and storage rooms. The hollow spaces, where building material was cut out, have an architectural quality. It is the negative counterpart of a positive space to be constructed elsewhere. By activating this space, the architects prove that there is no such thing as a useless space—even a hollowed-out space, which seems to be "nothing", can be reused and recycled.

Instead of drawing up plans, instead of subjecting matter to abstraction, the architects observe and register what is there. They approached the spaces "like explorers would do, equipped with the technology that expands our vision in the dark; by throwing millions of laser points on the wrinkles of the continuous stone surface, we register with millimetric precision the solid structure that was built for us and is now ready to be polished and inhabited".[7] The resulting images are striking. Instead of projecting what will be there, instead of drawing lines upon a tabula rasa, they register what is there and what will soon be the past. The ghostlike quality of the point-clouds, floating in a dark void like stars in a universe, results in a utopia of the past, as it were.

In the 20th century, the urban utopia took place in the air, a superstructure hovering and expanding over the surface of the city and the Earth. Ca'n Terra, meanwhile, expands into the ground. While the 20th-century utopias were about the space of the future, the empty medium to be filled, Ca'n Terra is about the past, the historical dimension that has been buried and cut off from the present. The walls embody the history of its former functions, industrial and military, but also the long history of the ground itself, i.e. the processes of sedimentation and transformation of matter.

As with The Truffle and the Structures of Landscape, Ca'n Terra challenges the traditional criteria of architecture. It is not easy to define an inside or an outside, or to clearly locate a "roof", or a "façade". The structures make us constantly

7 — Ensamble Studio, "Ca'n Terra", statement, undated, n.p.

change perspective and scale. The environment is either too big or too small, or, put differently, there is no such thing as a natural continuity between the scale of the human body and the non-human environment. And yet the architecture by Ensamble Studio demonstrates how one can inhabit the non-human, and adapt to its pre-existing niches, spaces, platforms and dimensions.

Experimental Spaces

Ensamble Studio have developed a very particular kind of architectural representation. Short videos with music—often by the composer and musician Antón García Abril, father of Antón García-Abril—depict the projects. Great emphasis is placed on the production process, either of the models or of the actual buildings. The time-lapse sequences of the architects and their collaborators working, pouring, cutting, moulding, cleaning, fixing, hammering and painting, all immediately inspire the observer to action. Lewis Mumford's idea about the origins of architecture being in the earth is pertinent here: "Mud and water, as children know, are plastic and responsive [...] The shaping of the earth was an integral part of the shaping of the city—and preceded it."[8]

Their videos are more than documentations. They are also manifestos. They demonstrate that the work of Ensamble Studio deals with the fundamentals of architecture without being fundamentalist, it deals with the essence of architecture without being essentialist. Whereas many people tend to go solemn when talking about the "essence of architecture", its "basis" and "foundations", these videos, which recall the silent movies from early cinema, are often comical.

The architecture of Ensamble Studio is experimental in the sense that it deals with what is not yet known. It demonstrates just how closely experimentation and playing are interrelated. This is why the model plays such a crucial role in the entire process. It allows for the testing of ideas, for reshuffling, for including hazards. It doesn't matter if a model collapses and an experiment fails. Like in a silent movie, where the protagonists get straight back up after falling over, there is always a next chance. A quote by Allan Kaprow, the artist who invented the "happening" in the late 1950s, comes to mind: "Experimental art is never tragic. It is a prelude."[9] The models are not abstractions of reality, but reality themselves. In the hands of Ensamble Studio, the separation between model and building no longer applies. They cross over the line between idea and realisation, plan and execution, the future and the present.

8 — Mumford, Lewis, *The City in History, Its Origins, Its Transformations, and Its Prospects*, New York: Harcourt, Brace & World, 1961, p. 17.

9 — Kaprow, Allan, "Experimental Art", in *Art News*, 65, no. 1, 1966. Reprinted in Kelley, Jeff (ed.), *Allan Kaprow. Essays in the Blurring of Art and Life*, Berkeley: University of California Press, 1993, p. 80.

Bjarke Ingels

I met Antón and Débora a decade ago, at an impromptu show-and-tell session for visiting professors at the Harvard Graduate School of Design (GSD). I had already encountered some of their work, namely in the form of the impossibly-large prefabricated concrete beams that greeted you at the Arsenale, during Kazuyo Sejima's Venice Biennale of Architecture in 2010. And I had also marvelled at their Hemeroscopium House on the outskirts of Madrid, which turned a seemingly academic exercise into a built reality. I had been wondering—how do you persuade a client to take such a vast leap of faith? Or get a contractor to build it? Turns out the answer is simple: you become the client, and the contractor.

We had been challenged to share a single project, in detail, with the other new faculty members. I brought with me our recent design for the Courtscraper (2012-2016)

Bjarke Ingels founded BIG – Bjarke Ingels Group in 2005 after co-founding PLOT Architects in 2001 and working at OMA in Rotterdam. Alongside his architectural practice, Bjarke has taught at Harvard University, Yale University, Columbia University, and Rice University and is an honorary professor at the Royal Academy of Arts, School of Architecture in Copenhagen. He is the author of *Yes is More* (Cologne, 2010) *and Big. Formgiving* (Cologne, 2020).

in New York, a hybrid of a European courtyard and an American skyscraper, and the reason (or at least the excuse) for my move to New York that same week. Antón shared a project he had just finished on the land of his summerhouse in Galicia: The Truffle, a tiny cabin, a kind of re-enactment of Le Corbusier's Cabanon, with identical proportions. And yet, there was a profound difference: the Cabanon is light, like furniture, and The Truffle is heavy, like a bunker, or even a boulder. There were other significant differences too, mostly around the complete inversion of the figure-ground: The Truffle was built by first stacking the space with hay bales, like Lego bricks—a solid representing the void. The bales were then encased in concrete by scooping up dirt on the sides, and forming a crater for the liquid cement around it. Finally, the two ends were cut away to open up an entrance and a window—a clean surgical cut in this grotesque organic form—much like a partially sliced truffle.

The entire construction process was orchestrated like a performance: the laying of the hay bales, the scraping of the dirt to make the outer formwork, the pouring of the concrete, the slicing of the sides. The excavation of the hay, freeing up the space inside, meanwhile, was performed by Paulina, the cow, all accompanied by a musical score courtesy of Antón's father, a composer. Even if somewhat insignificant in scale and scope—a guesthouse for their summer house—it was loaded with intention and meaning. Furthermore, it begged the question: where do you go from here? Is this an elegant exception, or could the underlying principles be taken further?

A few weeks later, they gave a talk on their entire oeuvre. It culminated in an almost megalomaniacal vision of a linear city that was simultaneously infrastructure and factory, to create itself, as much Ludwig Hilberseimer or Superstudio as Le Corbusier. I was fascinated how the same sensibility that had produced The Truffle could also create this more machine-like factory for cities. I wondered whether there might be an element of eclecticism or schizophrenia in play, but I have since come to realise that the opposite is in fact true.

There is perhaps a clue in their studio name: Ensamble ("assemble" in Spanish) is a clear play on words, alluding not only to how buildings are put together from their material and component parts, but also to the French word *ensemble* (a group of musicians) and the almost musical way in which the construction crew turns into a quasi-orchestra, enacting the architectural score in concert, as composed and directed by the architect-composer-conductor. This thinking is evidenced when you see the construction workers (often including Débora and Antón themselves, and their team) operating bulldozers, excavators and cranes in well-rehearsed moves, to the tune of musical scores. They are the only people I know who refer to rehearsals when talking about construction manoeuvres.

Balancing Act, installation at the Venice Architecture Biennale, Venice, 2010
© Roland Halbe

And this is key to what I believe sets them apart from almost any other practicing architects I know today. It is their obsession with the tectonics of construction: the choice of materials, the way they are put together and how the architecture is like the resultant residue left behind after the performance of construction has taken place. The material becomes like the instrument that ends up dictating what the architecture can be. Having followed them as their friend, colleague and admirer for exactly a decade now, I have seen how their almost fanatically persistent pursuits have led to a body of work that, paradoxically, is as wildly heterogenous as it is fundamentalistically consistent. Their projects seem to be along quite different paths or branches of exploration, but, ultimately, they all share the same sensibility, and they always end up converging in the most unexpected confluence of seemingly incompatible ideas.

Take The Truffle: the process of digging and scraping is frozen in time as the liquid concrete hardens, inheriting the imprint of a hollowed-out pit or a heaped pile of dirt. This has since taken them on a journey, designing and building structures such as their expressive landscape architecture in the Montana highlands, works that are distant cousins to Robert Smithson's *Spiral Jetty* or even Stonehenge. Casting their own boulders and leaning them against each other, forming gateways for giants. Or making a space out of earth, with little craters left for the concrete to form thick columns for holding the roof up—only to excavate the dirt and reveal the cavernous hall left behind. Or the Petrified River, where the architectural expression becomes like a found object that emerges through the performance of a preconceived process, instead of being imposed by an author. Their increasingly uninhibited material expressionism has even led to works made from concrete textile: wet sheets of concrete-laced cloth are solidified into furniture, and they look like the bastard children of Maarten Van Severen and Frank O. Gehry. The ultimate statement of this, for now, may well be the Calderona House, or its prototypical predecessor, built next to The Truffle, where they sprayed concrete onto canvas to create architectural forms, as if painted by concrete brushstrokes upon the fabric of space. As the expressionism becomes increasingly savage and unrestrained, the architecture—or at least its conventional functionality—recedes, shifting from the realm of architecture to that of sculpture.

Then you have the projects they built for the General Society of Authors and Publishers in Santiago de Compostela. One is a straightforward classic modernist structure that would be relatively inconspicuous were it not for the sourcing of the stone cladding. Rather than any conventional finish—polished, raw, bush hammered, etc.—the stones are left with the tectonic of a block freshly excavated from the quarry, including all the telltale drill lines left over from the process of wresting the chunk of rock from the mother mountain. They took this idea even further in the neighbouring pavilion, where they embraced the methodology of moving stones around like a giant toddler stacking up building blocks of rock. Rather than the conventional tools of the architect—the pen and paper, or the physical scale model—they went straight to full 1:1 scale, using excavators and cranes to balance a temple wall of leftover fragments of stone. It was more like playing than working—they arrived at a composition using the available kit of parts—and, once satisfied, they simply documented the design with photos and annotations on the rock, using the stone worker's haphazard orange spray lines to do so. And they then moved everything to the right spot. If the work in the quarry was the rehearsal, the construction became the inaugural and only performance.

These pursuits—the solids to voids, the building as resultant residue, the tectonics of quarries—have come together in Ca'n Terra, the ultimate architectural *objet trouvé*. Here, an abandoned stone quarry has been transformed into a home and workspace for the family/studio, with as little intervention as possible. Architectural drawings have been replaced by photomapped 3D scans. Finishes have been replaced by sanding, grinding and power washing to reveal the texture and material underneath. Rubble and dust have been solidified to form concrete floor slabs, and the walls are indistinguishable from the rocks they are made from. Skylights have been cut out, creating a Pantheon for troglodytes. Tarp and rebar have been combined to form an *architettura povera* revisit of the Maison de Verre. Ultimately, the commitment to the tectonics of construction—and the celebration of the revealing impact of the process on the product—has thus reached a climax, in which the main architectural expressions, the forms and flows of space, have in fact been created and left behind by the miners. The architects' impact is reduced to the pure art of appropriation.

A different branch of exploration can be seen in the Hemeroscopium House's use of ready-made mega beams, from the industry of prefabricated highway elements, using existing formworks where only the rebar is custom-made to serve the new purpose. Unable, as they were, to find a contractor for the job, they had to become their own contractor. There was no turning back after this decision. Since then, they have built every single building themselves. Architects create all kinds of documentation: drawings and models, images and mood boards, material samples and detail sections. Ultimately, they are all mere footnotes to inform and enable the construction workers to do the real work—to turn an abstract dream into concrete reality. Or, as Antón likes to say, "to translate data to matter" (in his Spanglish accent it actually rhymes). The built reality is the only goal, the only final outcome. All the work we do, all the media and models, all the data, they only exist as a stepping stone to get where we need to go, in the material world.

There are works before the Hemeroscopium House that inevitably led them there, and other works that followed on from it. The Reader's House in Matadero, Madrid, used concrete troughs like mega elements of furniture, intervening in an existing structure. The Berklee College of Music in Valencia would have been the

General Society of Authors and Publishers Headquarters, Santiago de Compostela, Spain, 2007
© Iwan Baan

application of these principles at scale. An unbuilt tower in Milan took Berklee to the vertical dimension. The Big Bang Tower and an entire family of towers that followed are all distant offspring of the Hemeroscopium House. In the process, even the models became ready-mades—the Styrofoam and cardboard were replaced by metal studs and paperclips (one day I visited them at home in the Hemeroscopium House, and the garden had turned into a storage unit for their models, like a hybrid of a sculpture garden and a scrapyard). The advantage of making your models exclusively out of concrete and galvanised metal is that you can in fact store them outdoors.

Since then, they have further pushed the idea of playing around with off-the-shelf products as ready-mades. They started experimenting with ultralight Styrofoam blocks to recreate the experience of the Hemeroscopium House, where space is the interstitial condition defined by monolithic elements. The limitations of the foam quickly revealed the need for something stronger, but that was still light: the metal stud.

The Cyclopean House is essentially creating heaviness out of lightness. Mega-girders are made from light metal studs, which are doubled, tripled, nested and layered to achieve the required strength. The concrete walls are replaced by fibre cement board. They were prefabricated and built by their own team in Spain, then shipped to Boston to be erected there, at a fraction of the time and cost it would have taken to build them on site. A studio in Madrid followed, in the form of galvanised fundamentalism: walls, floors, shelves, tables and benches, all made from the same studs.

Ultimately, all of these experiments—of lightness and heaviness, of the extraordinary use of ordinary products—led to what may be their wildest undertaking so far. In an industrial polygon in a Madrid suburb, a factory has been built from what appears to be galvanised metal studs and polycarbonate. Upon closer inspection, however, you realise that the columns are in fact concrete, even if clad in sheet metal. Or rather cast, not clad. By combining the benefits of light prefabricated elements (for ease of transportation and manoeuvring) with the benefits of heavy in-situ concrete (for resilience and strength), they have created something with the best of both worlds. Prefabricated ultralight elements that will serve as the conduit for concrete poured inside. Formwork that stays behind as the finish. The factory is built to make more of itself. Or, at least, more buildings out of the same system that it helped evolve by means of its own construction.

Over the last quarter of a century, while the entire world of manufacturing has seen a steady increase in productivity, the construction industry has flatlined, if not declined. The absence of automation and additive manufacturing has prevented the built environment from benefitting from the technologies that are now making our cars and smartphones of ever-higher quality, at steadily lower costs. Regardless of how sophisticated our documentation has become with CAD and BIM, when the rubber hits the road, when data is translated to matter, the innovation ends. With WoHo (World Homes), Ensamble are combining all their discoveries from two decades of radical experimentation, and turning it all into a systemic, holistic approach to the entire industry.

Like Apple's integration of software and hardware, WoHo promises to integrate data and matter (i.e. architecture and construction), thereby increasing quality and innovation, and bringing down construction time and cost.

In the process, the studio has moved into the factory—it seems like the logical outcome when you start using a crane to make models and a concrete gun to sketch. In their unique form of systemic expressionism, Antón and Débora have made an impressive body of work, which has made great impact—this alone is enough to justify their significant position in the ongoing conversation we call architectural history. However, and more importantly, all these seemingly separate experiments accumulate into something that might actually constitute a major breakthrough, all in a construction industry that is resistant (if not outright immune) to innovation. To do so, the architects have become builders, and their studio, a factory. Having been with them on their journey over the last decade, I am full of anticipation—hope, in fact—for the industry, for the profession, for the art, in terms of what may come of this new and fully integrated hybrid practice.

Perhaps the secret to their knack for blending data and matter, design and construction, practice and academia, is in the way they approach their own lives. As frequent guests in their home(s), my family and I have had front-row seats to observe how they live and breathe what they do. Whereas contemporary life coaches preach disciplines of separation in order to achieve a healthy work-life balance, Antón and Débora have turned their own lives into a living, working laboratory. They have lived their own creations, and they have tested and tasted the benefits and side effects of every imaginable tectonic and material. As have their friends, I am happy to report. Ultimately, I think this may partly explain why they manage to surpass most architects in the reach of their dreams and the radicality of their experimentation. They have turned their own lives into a single, massively vertically-integrated stack—this includes dreaming, designing, building, working and living their own experiments. Step one for mastering how to translate data into matter, the ideal into the real, is to practice what you preach. As far as I'm concerned, Débora and Antón are the very incarnation of their own ideals.

Hemeroscopium House, Madrid

2005-2008

For the ancient Greeks, the *hemeroscopium* was the place where the sun sets, an allusion to somewhere that exists only in our mind, in our senses, a place that is ever-changing and mutable, but is nonetheless real. It is delimited by the scope of the horizon, by the physical limits set by the light, and it emerges over time.

This house encompasses a domestic space and a distant horizon, and it does so by playing around with seemingly unbalanced structures that enclose the living spaces and draw vision outwards. Bold, heavy structures are laid out in such a way that provokes the gravitational action that moves the space, and the whole place is thus defined.

The order in which these structures are stacked generates a helix which juts out from a stable support, the main beam, and it develops upwards in a sequence of increasingly light elements—seven in total—before closing at a point that caps off this system of equilibrium. The design of their joints responds to their constructive nature, to their forces, while their stresses show the structural condition. Given the way that this structure is set, the house becomes airy, light, transparent, and the space inside flows with life. The apparent simplicity of the structure's joints in fact required complex calculations, due to the reinforcement and the pre-tension and post-tension of the steel rods that bind the beams.

It took us a year to engineer this structure but only seven days to build it, thanks to the total prefabrication of the different elements and a perfectly coordinated assembly. All of our efforts went into developing the technique that would allow us to create a very specific space. And thus, an astonishing new language is invented, where form disappears, giving way to the naked space. The epitome of the equilibrium in Hemeroscopium House is embodied in what we ironically call the "G-spot", a twenty-ton granite stone that serves as an expression of the force of gravity, and a physical counterweight to the whole structure.

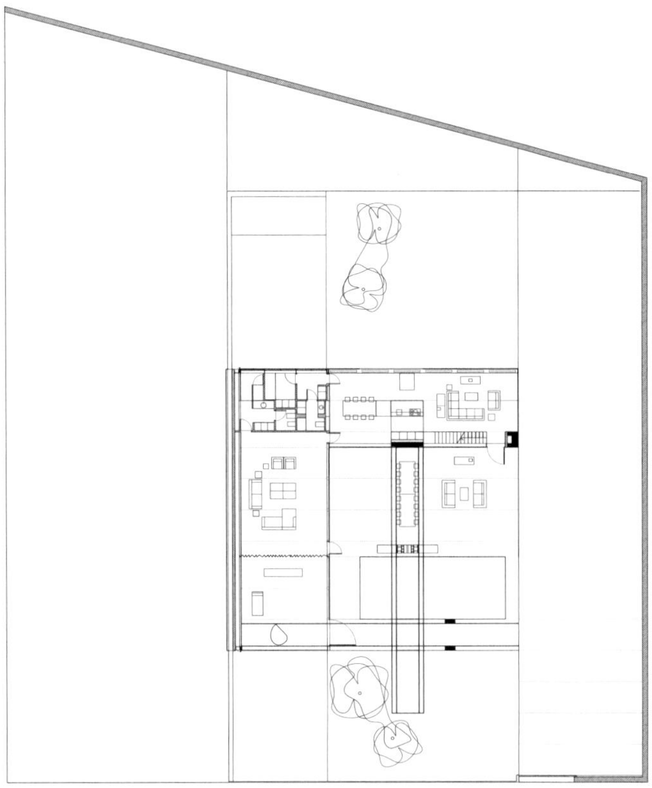

Plan level +3.07 m

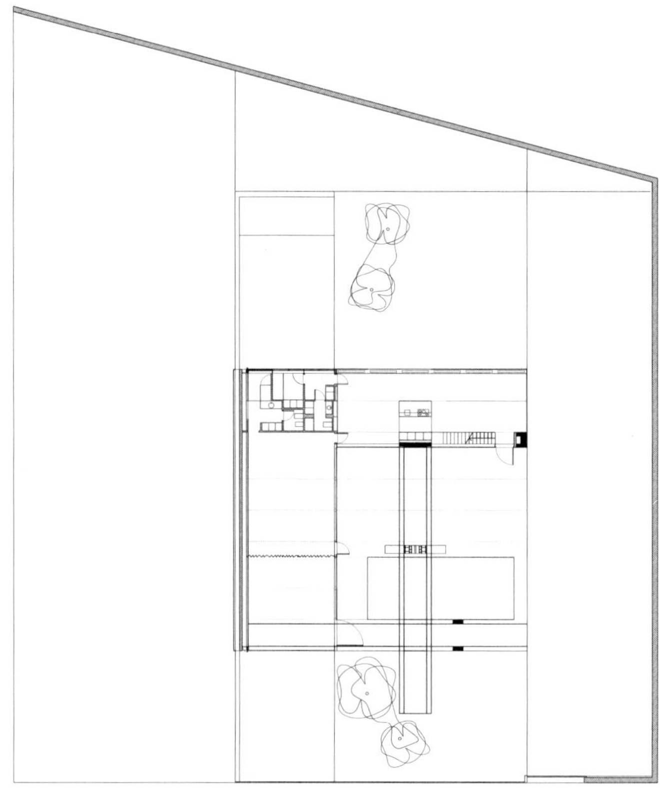

Plan level +3.07 m

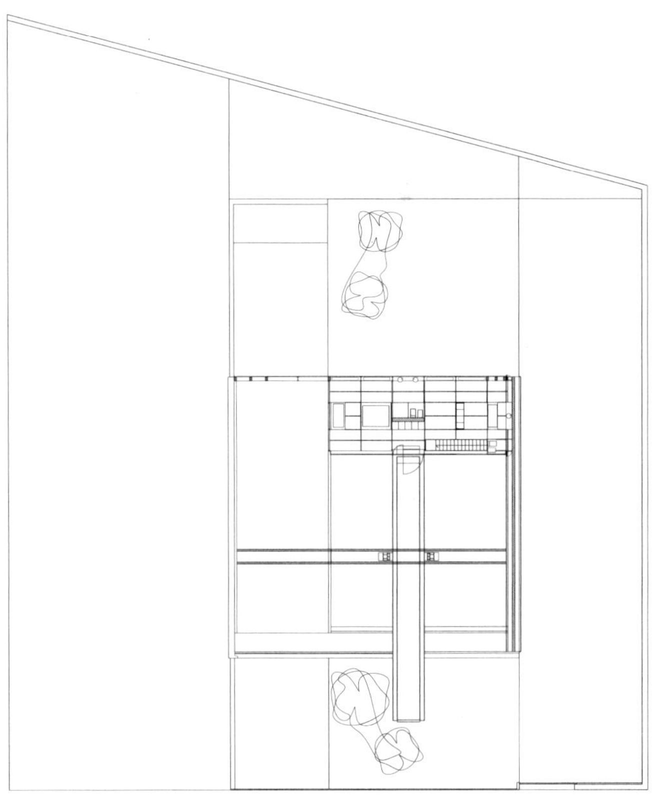

Plan level +6.32 m

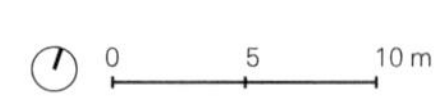

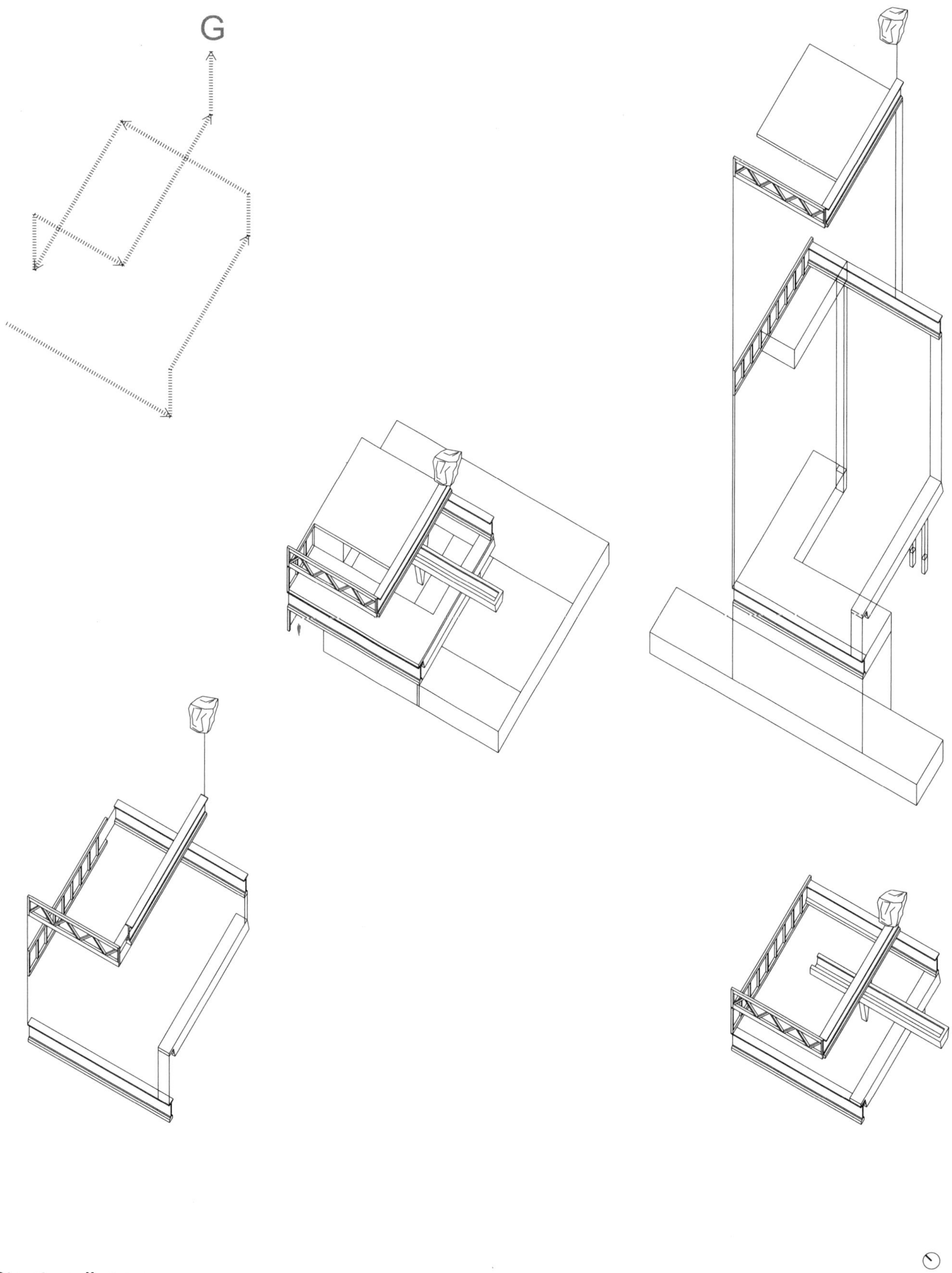

Structure diagram

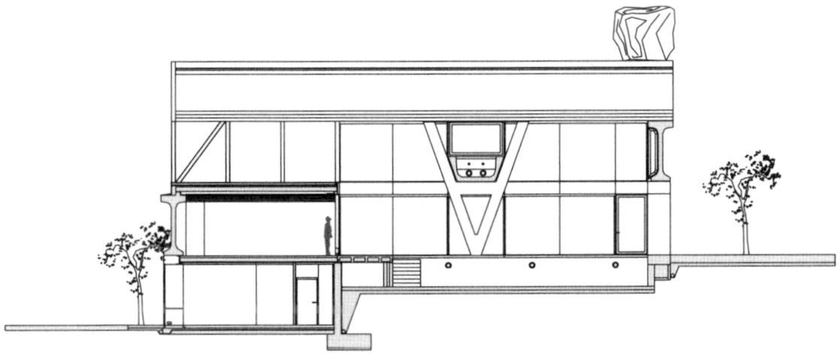

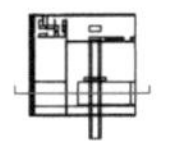

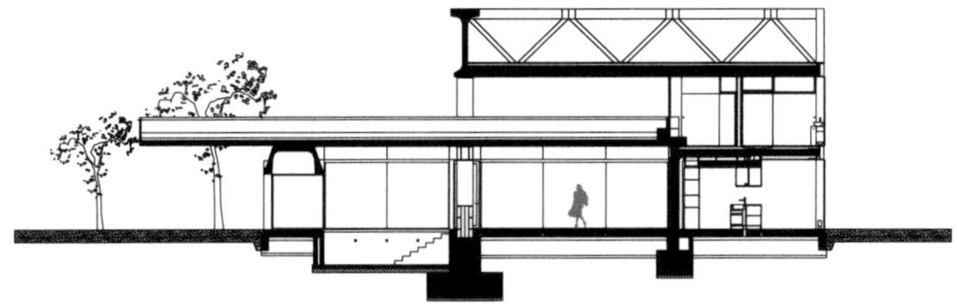

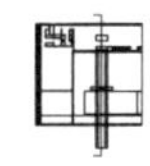

Cross-sections

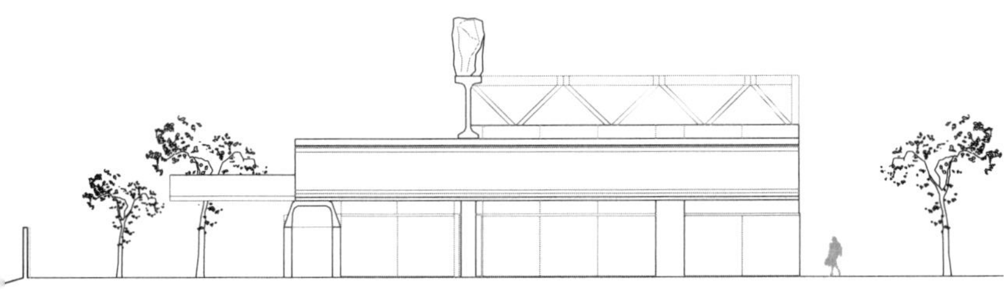

East elevation

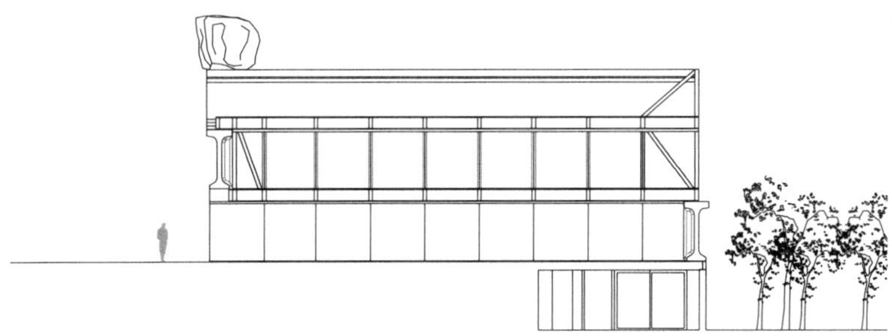

North elevation

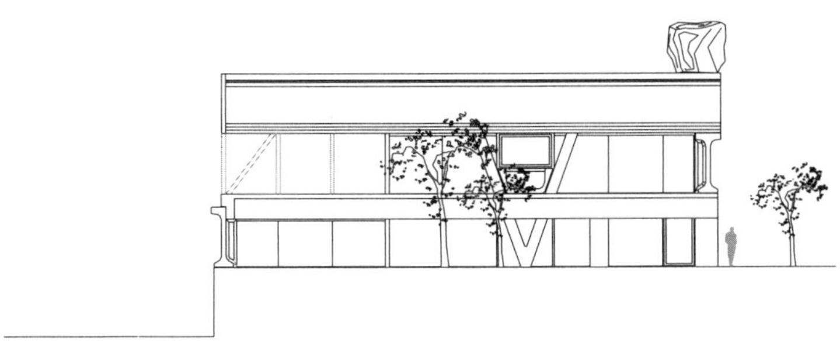

South elevation

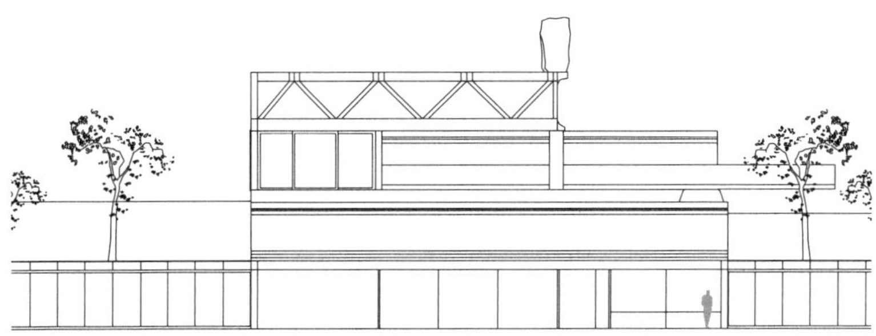

West elevation

0 5 10 m

The Truffle, Costa da Morte

2006-2010

The Truffle is a piece of nature built with earth, and full of air. It is a space within a stone on the ground, blending into the territory. It camouflages itself by emulating the processes of mineral formation in its own structure, and it integrates with the natural environment by obeying its laws.

To build it, we made a hole in the ground, then we piled around its perimeter the topsoil we had removed—this way, we formed a retaining dike, one without any mechanical consistency. Then, we materialised the air by building a mound of hay bales, before flooding the space between the earth and the constructed air, so that it would solidify. The poured mass concrete enveloped the air, protected by the ground. Time passed, and we removed the earth, to reveal an amorphous mass.

The earth and the concrete had swapped properties. The earth provided the concrete with its texture and colour, its form and essence, while the concrete gave the earth its strength and internal structure. But, at this point, what we had created was not architecture—we had made a stone.

Using quarry machinery, we made a few cuts to reach the core and expose the hay inside, which had now been compressed by the hydrostatic pressure that the concrete had exerted on the flimsy vegetal structure. To hollow out the interior, Paulina the calf came along, and she enjoyed 50 m^3 of the most delicious food, which she fed on for a year until she left her habitat, now an adult and weighing 300 kg. The interior volume had been eaten away, and the space thus appeared for the first time, restoring the architectural condition of The Truffle, after having been a shelter for the animal and the vegetable mass for so long.

The resulting architecture surprised us. There was great ambiguity between the natural and the constructed, and also in the complex materiality that the same constructive element—the unreinforced concrete mass—could provide this small architectural space, at different scales: from the shapeless texture of its exterior, to the violent incision of a deep cut that reveals its architectural calling, to the fluid expression of the interior solidification of the concrete.

This dense materiality, which gives the vertical walls a rusticated scale, comes from the size of the bales. It contrasts with the continuous liquidity of the ceiling that evokes the sea, petrified in the lintel of the spatial frame that overlooks, sublimely, the Atlantic Ocean. The horizon is thus highlighted as the only tense line of the interior space.

To provide the space with all the comfort and the living conditions needed in architecture, we took Le Corbusier's Cabanon as a motif, recreating its programme and dimensions. It is the reference to the Cabanon of Beton that makes The Truffle such an enjoyable living space within nature, one which has inspired us.

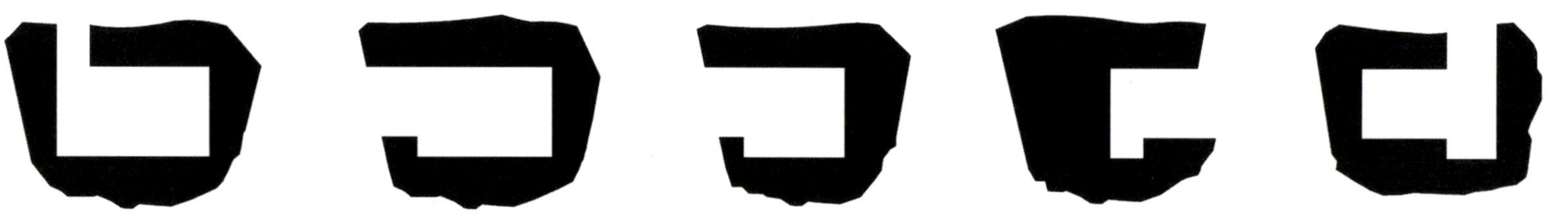

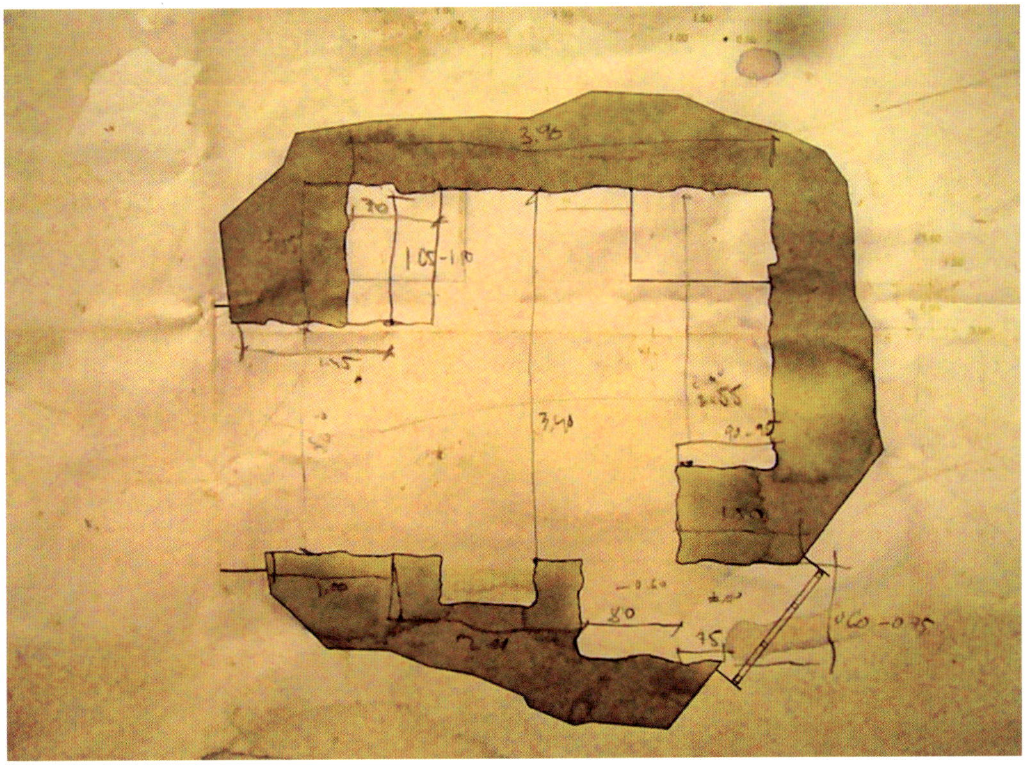

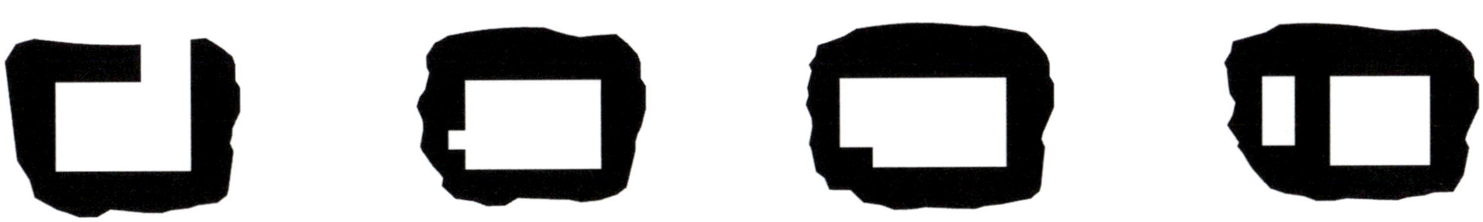

The Truffle, Costa da Morte

Reader's House, Madrid

2006-2012

The Reader's House is a place for education and innovation, a place where reading is understood as an active creative process that can be implemented in an immense variety of ways, reading books being just one of them. To create the space for such an ambitious project, Madrid's Matadero, the old slaughterhouse, with its 148,300 m^2 dedicated to contemporary creation, as well as its unique architectural presence, turned out to be the perfect site. Within this historic complex, the Reader's House occupies warehouses 13, 14, 17b and 17c, to hold cultural and educational events and activities—which occupy its key spaces—as well as an administrative area and a multifunctional auditorium.

This protected architectural complex required surgical precision to retain its appearance and internal structure, while providing the framework for the new use. In order to bring about this transformation, the consolidation of the pre-existing structure—which was in a precarious state, in terms of stability—was followed by the insertion of a new structure, and thus a new order, in close dialogue with one of the original buildings.

This new order is built by bridges—40-ton and 23-metre precast concrete beams—which are inserted through the windows of the thick masonry walls and allowed to rest on them. They cross the basilica-like space of the twin buildings, 13 and 14, without intermediate supports, to link transversally what used to be independent spatial units. These architectural elements symbolically represent the spirit of the project, i.e. the act of communication, one of the new programme's aims. They also physically resolve the connection between the warehouses, and, structurally, they become raised walkways that offer an additional space for the activity therein.

Two physical, perceptual and functional levels are defined, configuring thus a mutable setting. The lower level is open, dynamic, social, easily accessible from the street and dedicated to exhibitions and academic group activities. The upper level is a space for more private research and study, visually connected to the larger space of the original buildings but sheltered by the inserted linear structures.

This project respects and enhances the original character of the industrial and monumental complex. The delicate interior metal structure, and the masonry perimeter wall that defined the historic containers, today continue to define it, and the confluence and relationship between both architectures—old and new—succeed in preserving the memory of the place, while its life continues to bustle with new stories.

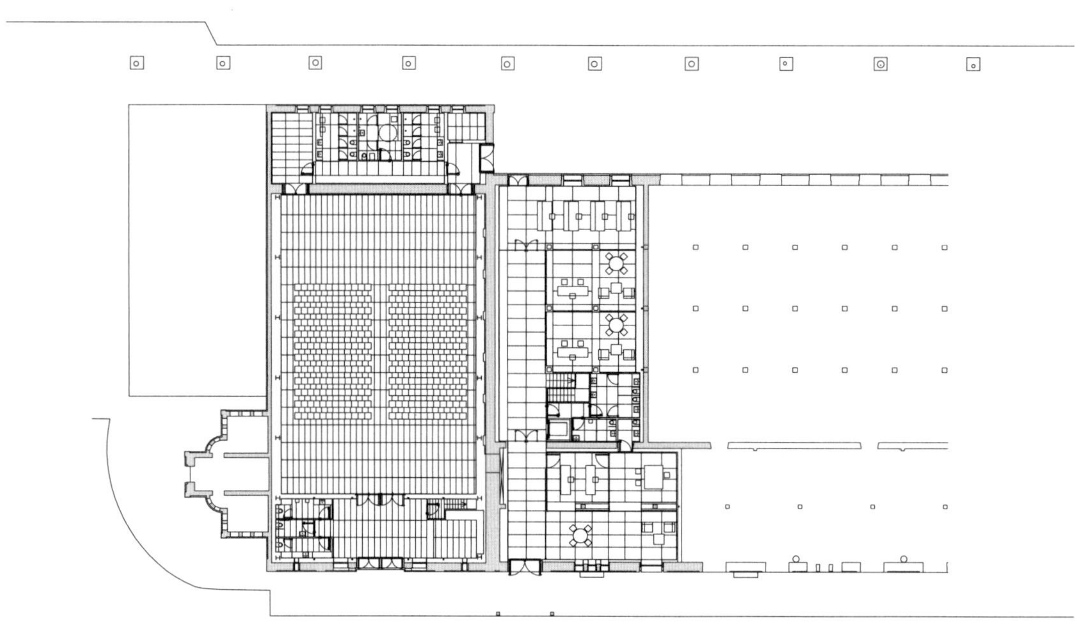

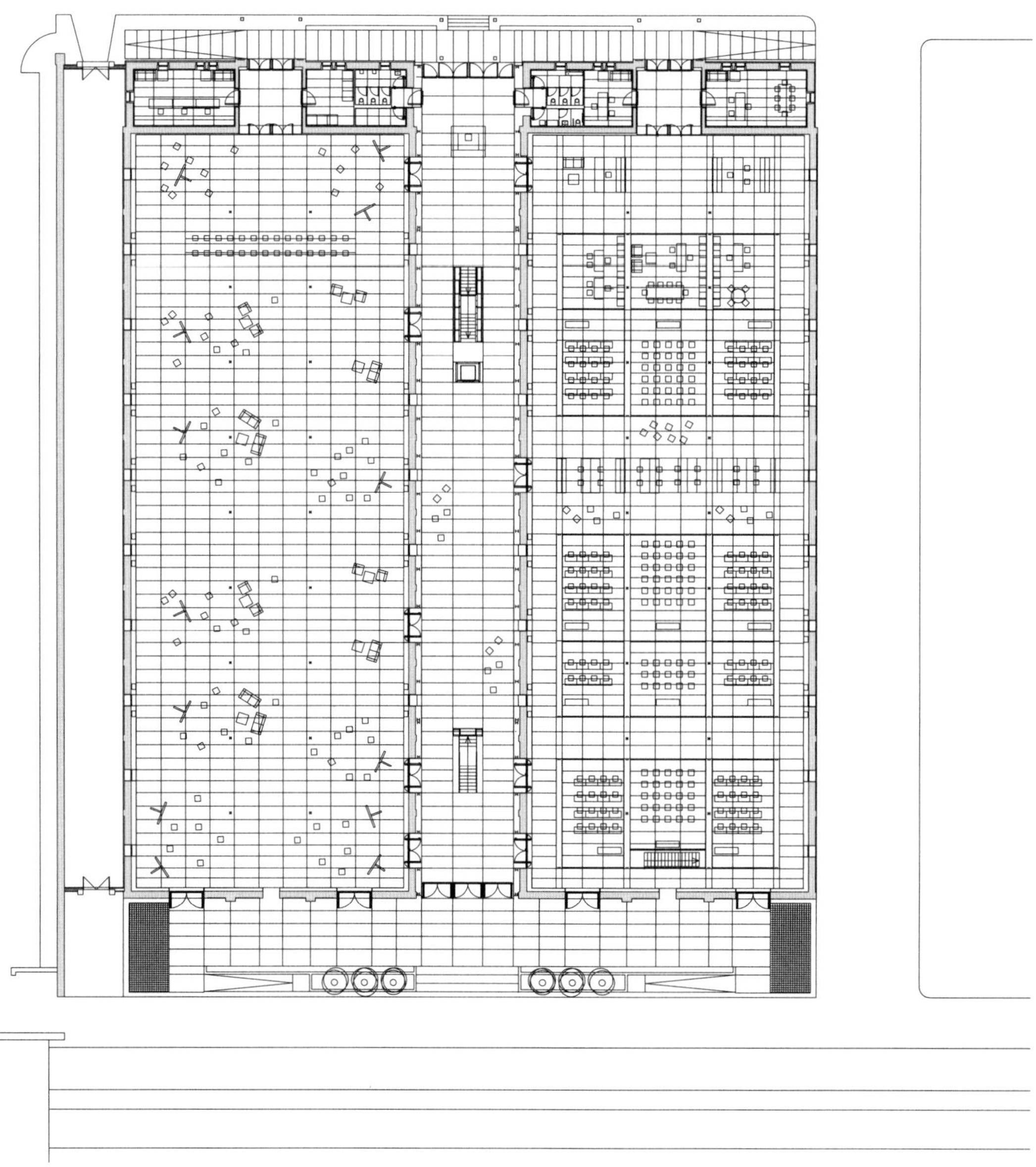

Ground floor

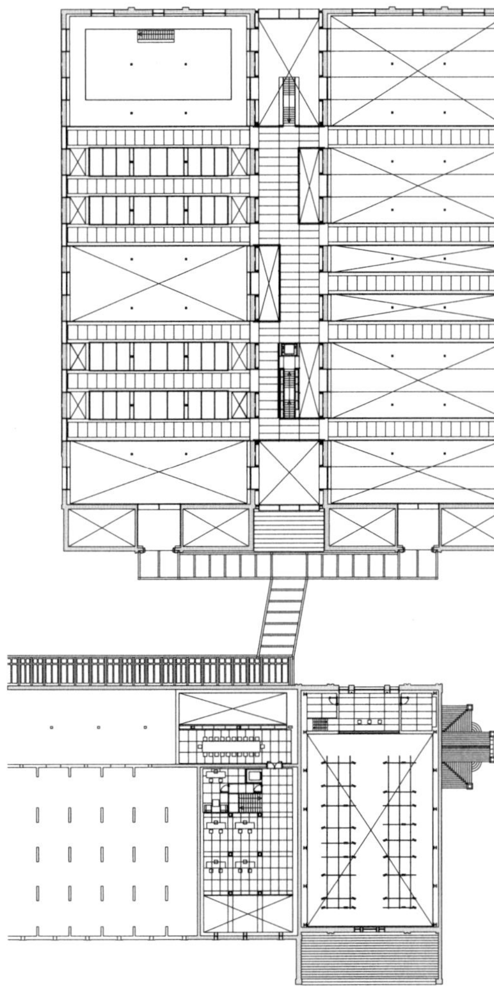

Mezzanine

0 5 10 m

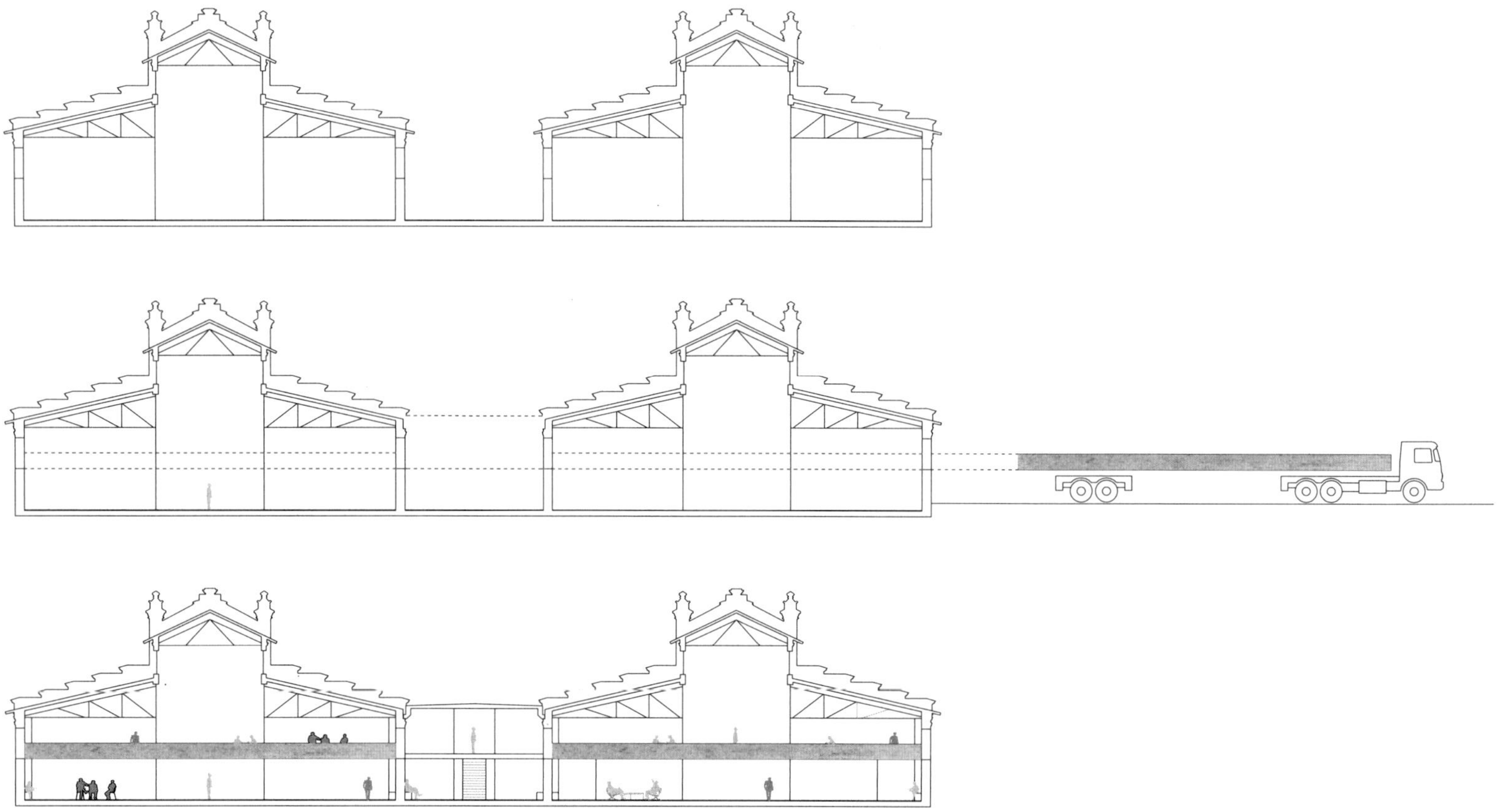

Cross-section

CASA DEL LECTOR

NU
BE
AU
LA

Telcel Theatre, Mexico City

2007-2012

Telcel Theatre, buried underground, features a large, bold metallic structure that rises above the ground level. This part is called the Dovela, the keystone, and it acts as bait to lure people in. We understand contemporary culture as the constant expression of connection with the movements of the time, so the layers of history that overlap and hybridise with Mexican culture are of great inspiration when making a work of architecture today. With this in mind, the Dovela appears as a stone of air, held up by the space formed from a sequence of excavated terraces. It engages with the sun, which tells the time as its rays peek through the slats, and it protects us from the rain and shelters us inside the earth. The Dovela tries to take in all the resonances of the world that reach it, and put them in order. It is a mathematical object that allows the natural elements (water, light and air) to have a bearing on its ultimate configuration. The excavated spaces, realised as a sequence of theatre lobbies at different levels, are given over to the public and are opened up to the sky, all protected by the symbolic metal structure.

The project contrasts the two fundamental principles with which it was built: the deep density of the negative space, which is vertical in nature, and the horizontal tension of the air contained and supported by the Dovela. The latter is the final key piece of an abstract balancing, and it seems to shed its weight in order to appear airy, mutable and light, just like a cloud that affects the space on the ground by blocking the sunlight. This contact between the sun and the earth, though, would not be able to discern any pattern in the order of the rays. As such, in the design of the structure that forms the gravitational connection between the Dovela and the excavations in the ground, we decided on a very figurative solution, as if they were caryatids and atlantes. This evokes diversity, reflecting the world of whoever will occupy the space. Therefore, the supports take part in the movement, in time, and they freely join in with this spatial dance, while their non-symmetrical disposition relies on the strength of the structure within the internal grid of the Dovela.

By immersing ourselves in the negative space of the open excavated lobbies, we can access a new and final happening. Once inside the earth, the theatre appears as the end of this sequence of spaces. Here, the synthesis of the building culminates with the function of a time that is frozen, recreated: a place for contemplation.

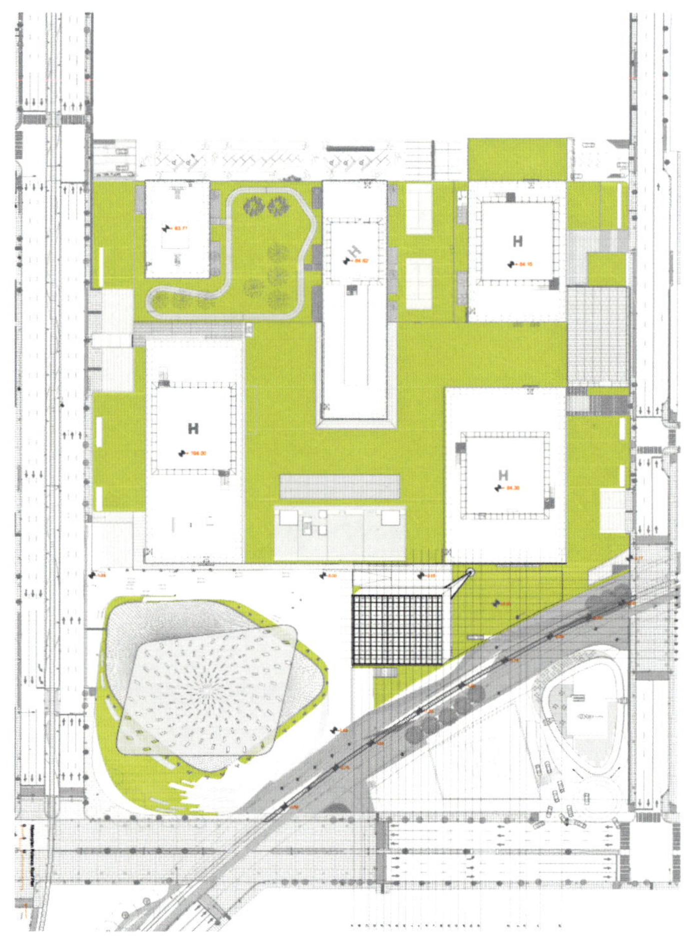

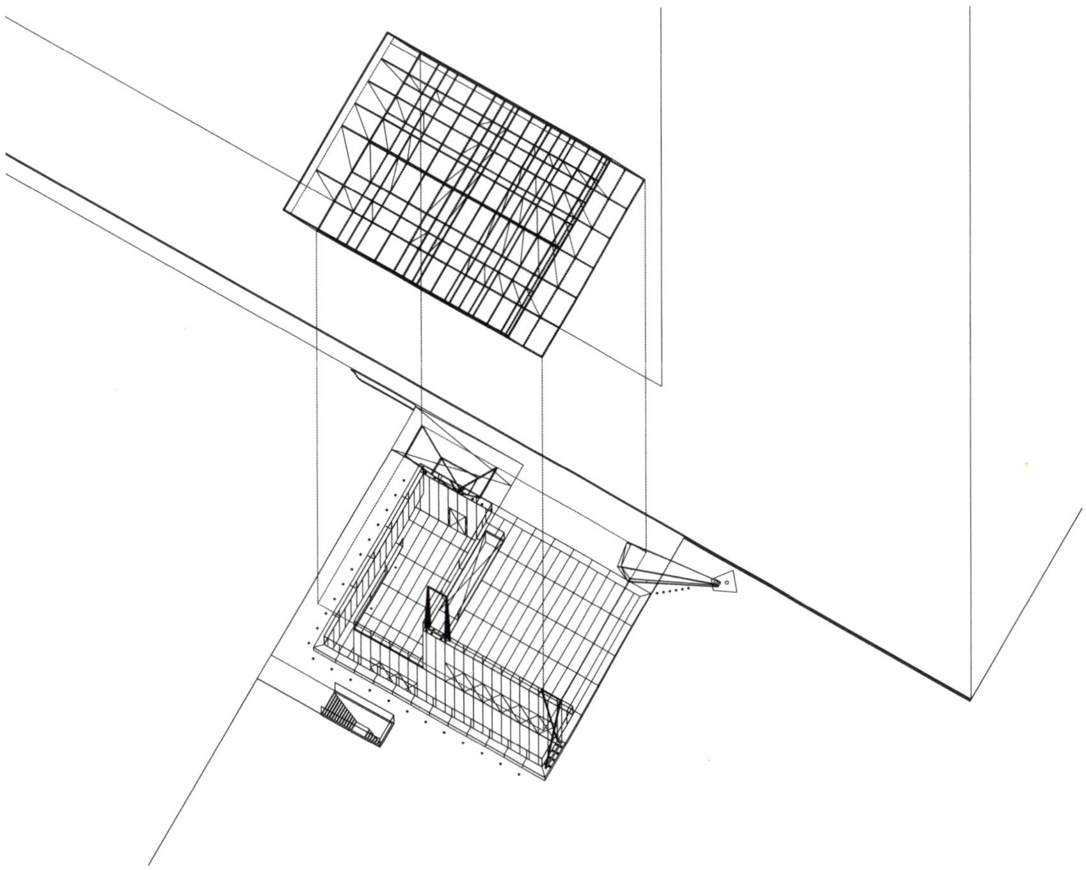

Telcel Theatre, Mexico City

Cyclopean House, Brookline, Massachusetts

2014-2015

Cyclopean House is built with the brute strength of the builder and the ingenuity of the engineer. It sets off on a journey from where it is manufactured—Madrid—to its definitive home on top of an existing garage, the ugly duckling of a quiet residential neighbourhood in Brookline, Boston. The gloomy, one-story construction accommodates the car park, workshop and service spaces, following its own basic structural logic. It is then completed with a big room built on top of it, via the assembly of the large prefabricated elements that come to rest there after a long transatlantic voyage. This open-plan, double-height living area includes the main domestic activities, and it enables the transformation of this residual building into a two-story residential unit, which is technologically and spatially adapted to the life of its users.

The new architecture concentrates the structure and infrastructure into the perimeter. There are seven monumental beams, which each entail a different action: cooking & bathing, storing, seating, dining, sleeping, working, projecting. The rest of the plan is then cleared, to be shared by different events taking place at any given time, while varying functions can expand into the central space as needed, defining thus a temporary layout. The seven programmatic beams make up a thick enclosure that minimises visual contact with the exterior on the three sides overlooked by the neighbouring houses, and in turn there is a large opening onto the street side, through which the interior space can contemplate the trees opposite, and imagine itself in the middle of a park. As well as this one huge eye, beams interlock to embrace the space, and they seem less dense at contact points where edges slot together and connections are pushed back, in order to provide additional light and ventilation for specific functions. Privacy and thermal insulation are thus guaranteed, while maximising light and the view.

To avoid overloading the pre-existing structure or having to dig new foundations, ultra-light construction systems were used to shape the new elements. These were solid foam cores —98% air—which were reinforced by steel profiles, and fire-proofed with a thin layer of cement and fibres. Dry joints and the material's lightness enable the different elements to be produced offsite, including the fixtures and fittings. They were then easily transported by ship and lorry, and quickly pieced together following a perfectly-timed sequence that was carefully planned in advance.

Unlike the heavy, cold stone that prevented Ulysses from leaving the cave, Cyclopean House is light and warm—light due its lack of mass, and warm due to its cosy coat of air. It sits and watches without being seen, its elements interlaced after their own odyssey.

BOSTON
MADRID
A5368

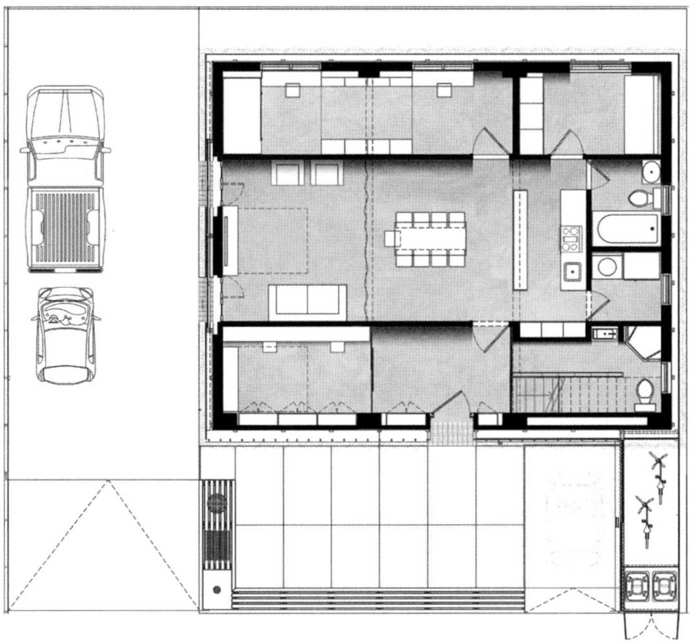

Ground floor

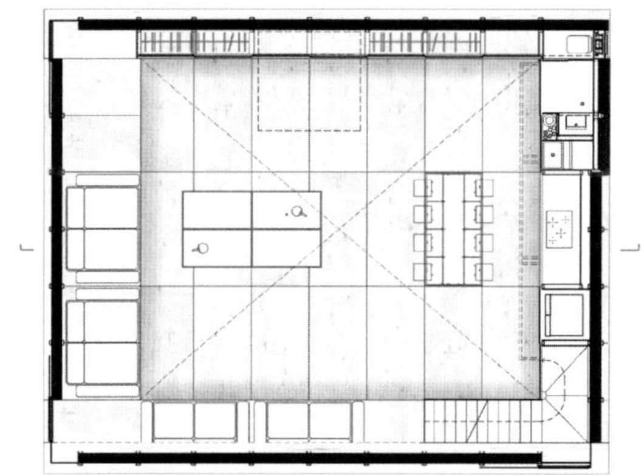

First floor

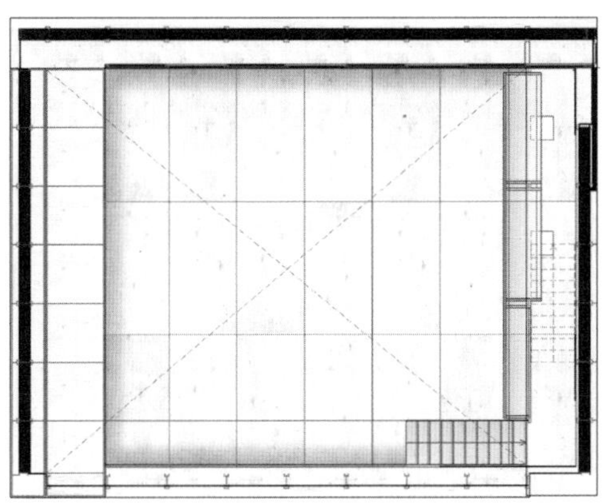

Mezzanine

Roof floor

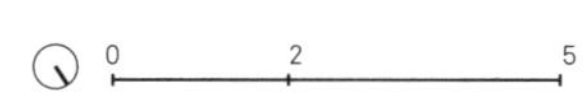

Cross-section

Longitudinal section

South elevation

North elevation

West elevation

East elevation

37

UNIVERSAL
AN MCA COMPANY

BOLTS
4

Structures of Landscape, Fishtail, Montana

2014-2016

Located at the edge of Yellowstone Park in Montana, Tippet Rise Art Center—set amid over 4,500 hectares of wilderness—was born as a new destination for the arts, in which musical performances and large-scale outdoor sculptures would play a major role.

How the current local fauna and ranching activity can coexist with the added artistic and architectural interventions is a challenge that the project needs to embrace. This kind of challenge has fuelled the research that started with our early activity in the quarry, and continued with experiments such as The Truffle. These experiences advanced our knowledge and appreciation of what pre-existing natural conditions can offer us, both as architects and as users of architecture.

Once again, we go back to primary elements in order to configure site-specific architectures that are in harmony with nature. By working with earth and rocks, and learning from their formation logics, different techniques and processes are developed to manipulate the structural, acoustic and thermal properties of these local materials at different scales. Also, geological transformation processes—sedimentation, erosion, weathering, crystallisation, compaction, metamorphism—are reinterpreted to cultivate structures that are made of the landscape itself. These structures take existing matter and reinforce it, using highly engineered processes while embracing unpredictable results. The resulting forms have been twinned with those removed from the land that previously contained and supported them, from which they retain the memory and imprint, affording them thus new meaning and tension. They are structures of landscape because they are born from it and give it order, transforming matter into inhabitable space, and they allow a new constellation of programmes to take place among the site's plateaus, ridges, canyons and hills of brutal beauty.

The Structures of Landscape enable habitation without exploitation, and they encourage close relationships with the environment. They resonate with the immensity, the roughness, the silence and the magical solitude of the place, while amplifying its qualities, and situating our actions in an ambiguous position that lies somewhere between nature, architecture and art. They might be one or all of these things, or even a completely different category that only makes sense right there, as and when it happens.

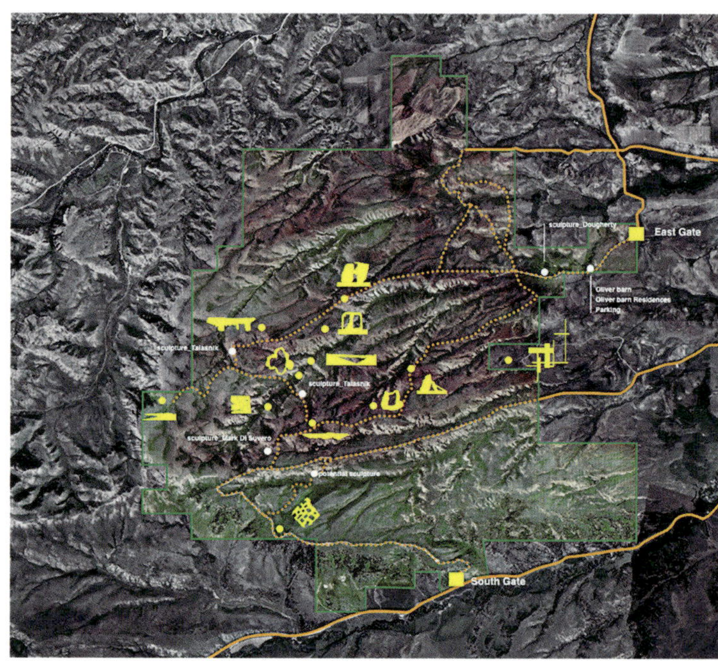

DOMO

Structures of Landscape, Fishtail, Montana

Structures of Landscape, Fishtail, Montana

Structures of Landscape, Fishtail, Montana

Structures of Landscape, Fishtail, Montana

Baldacchino

Reticula

Ponte

Midnight rostra

Tempietto

Auspicatum

Fontana

Tabula rasa

Zig Zag House, San Martín de Valdeiglesias

2015-2017

Zig Zag House slides down the slope between the trees. Its structures are attached to the ground while it tumbles towards the water in a cascade of spaces, which are linked together but still enjoy their own unique position on the site. By minimising its footprint, the house tip-toes along the ground, and its beams stick out like stones in a giddy balancing of precarious horizontality, where the life of the house develops in a constant movement between shifting forms. Each level offers a space, but there are no rooms. Each level offers a different outlook, but there are no windows. Each level offers a different way to experience the landscape, with the forest as the backdrop. The brushstrokes of the house's and trees' structures together draw out the zigzag space, without touching each other. They dance together, while keeping a respectful distance. And the inertia of the sloping terrain pushes everything downwards: the structures resist this thrust because they are tightly anchored to the ground, but the space flows until it plunges deep into the water of the San Juan reservoir.

The ambition to live in the air and only gently touch the earth, floating over it until reaching the water, led us to design the construction of Zig Zag House with lightweight materials, ones that delicately settle on the site, from bottom to top, going against the flow.

Roof Floor +3.00

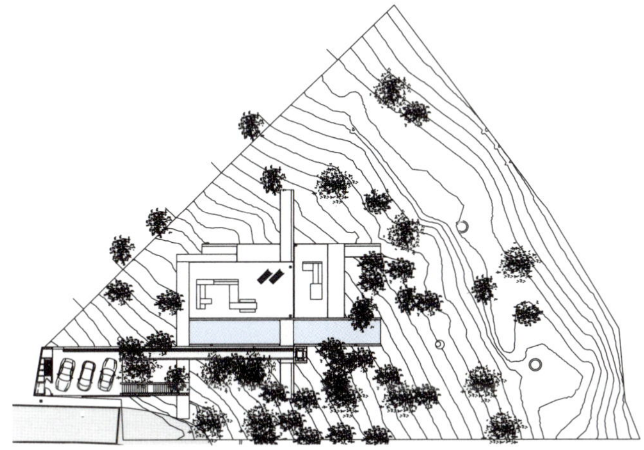

Floor Level +0.00

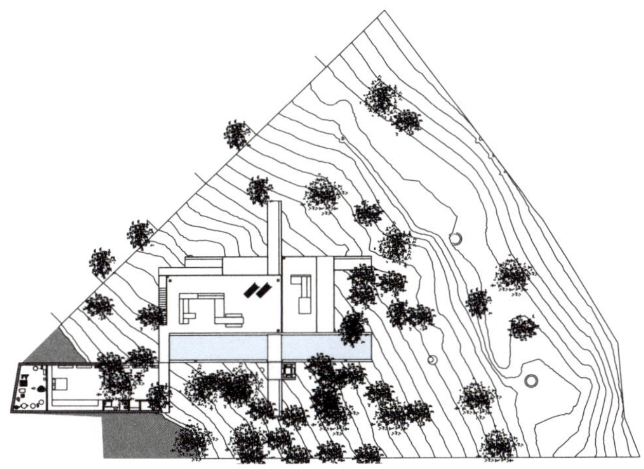

Floor Level -3.35

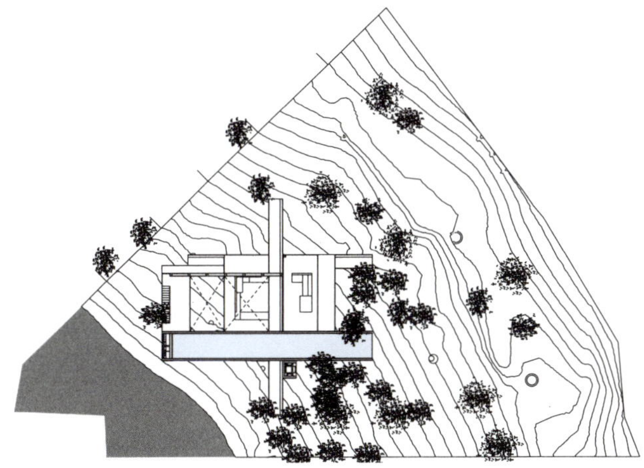

Floor Level -6.95

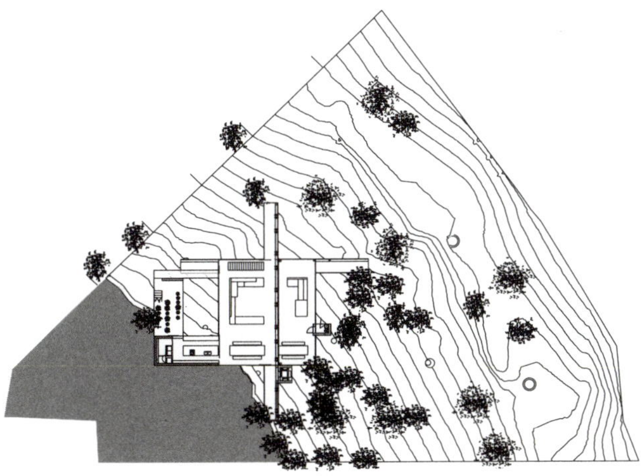

Floor Level -10.25

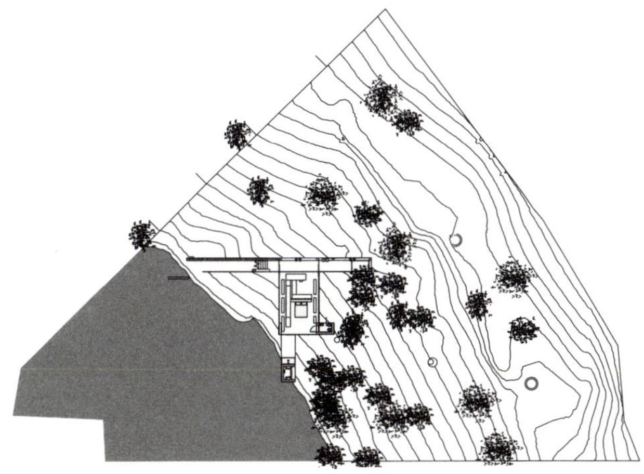

Ground floor -12.57

0 10 20 m

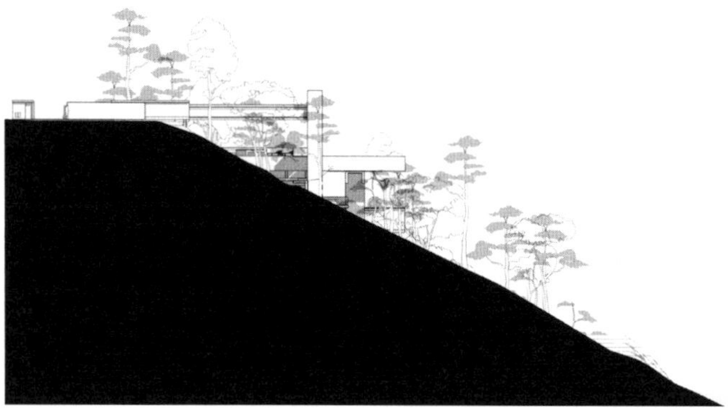

South Elevation

East Elevation

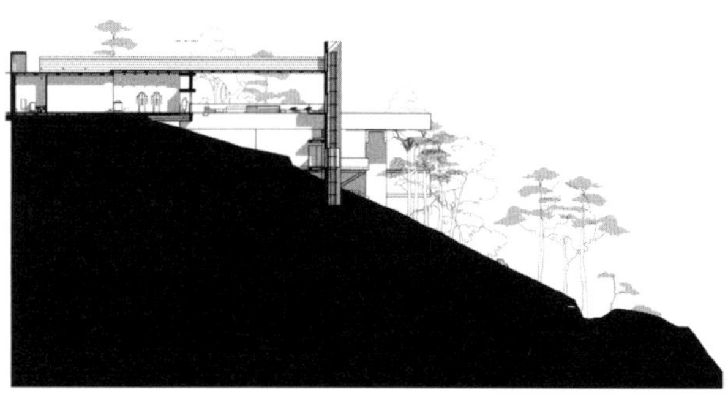

Section

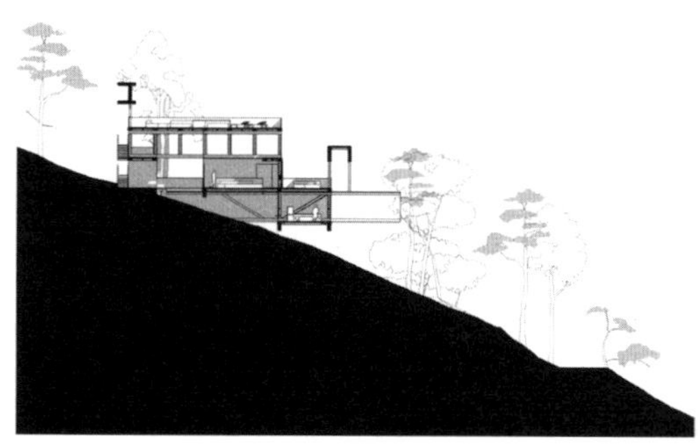

Section

Towers of Landscape

2016-2017

During our experiences designing and building Structures of Landscape, we learned a lot about the magnetic relation between people and spaces of nature: the spaces that embody nature, that enact nature, or that simply refer to it in pertinent ways. Because of the roughness of natural spaces, and their wilderness, their low resolution, their constant transformation, their connection with the essential and their disconnection with urban environments, their inexactness that so liberates the spirit and sparks the imagination... or perhaps even all of the above, we are inherently attracted to such spaces, structures, and images.

The Structures of Landscape, as we first envisioned them, emerge from and resonate with the landscape where they are located—they become embedded in the larger systems and constellations of elements that provide context and meaning. This research still makes us wonder whether it is possible to partially displace such experience, and operate in the city with some of the lessons learnt. This might be a countermovement whereby "nature" is built anew, so it can take up some of the spaces otherwise reserved for efficient industrialised structures. In these spaces, the borders between the natural and the artificial would be blurred, and architecture would be allowed to refer to the space of the mountains, the canyons, the cliffs and the caves.

MELTED

LAYERED

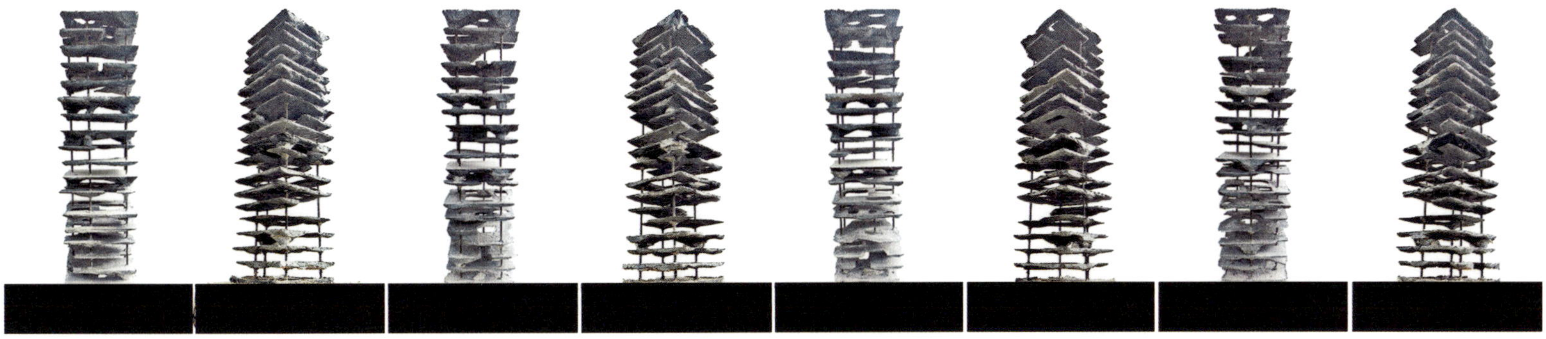

RETICULATED

Big Bang Tower, Chicago

2016-2017

Revisiting this *Chicago Tribune* competition makes us speculate about the requirements of contemporary office programmes, and also the role of the skyscraper in the city. In our contemporary culture, working spaces can no longer be understood as the fixed cubicles where workers spend the whole day immersed in their own particular task, progressively accumulating piles of paper that will require the equivalent amount of physical storage. A paradigm shift is underway, greatly enabled by information technologies: new avenues are being opened up for the re-imagining of these spaces and their demands. Today, an office can be a cubicle and also an open coworking area, it can be a cafe, a lounge, a lab, a multipurpose room, a virtual substance in the cloud, a room in your house and much more. This diversification—and enrichment—of the meaning of "office" gives us the opportunity to think about architecture in renewed urban terms, especially when the structure that supports such a diversity of functions is a tower with a vast physical presence.

Big Bang Tower embraces the scale of the city and the need for transformation in its programmes. By exploding the typical central core of a conventional high-rise building, and locating the fragmented parts in the envelope, access to the stacked floors is multiplied. The thick, asymmetrical columns adapt to the requirement of the server spaces to resolve both the vertical structure and the infrastructure, i.e. everything the space needs to facilitate activity. The rest is open space: open to the requirements of an increasingly diverse programme, open to the changing of these requirements over time, open to exciting connections with the public realm of the city. The convenient shell and core concept, that was developed for modern office buildings, is here given new spatial scale and quality, ensuring a more stimulating experience. The horizontal structures that tie the perimeter columns together contribute to this by each having a different position, area and height, so that the activity is not contained identically in every level, which in turn leads to manifold ways of framing the city and connecting interior spaces.

This column of columns, that learns from history and reframes the context of the *Chicago Tribune* competition, is not dismissive of the competition's goal to design "the world's most beautiful office building". It looks for this beauty in the thorough revision of the typology, and in its relation to the urban context.

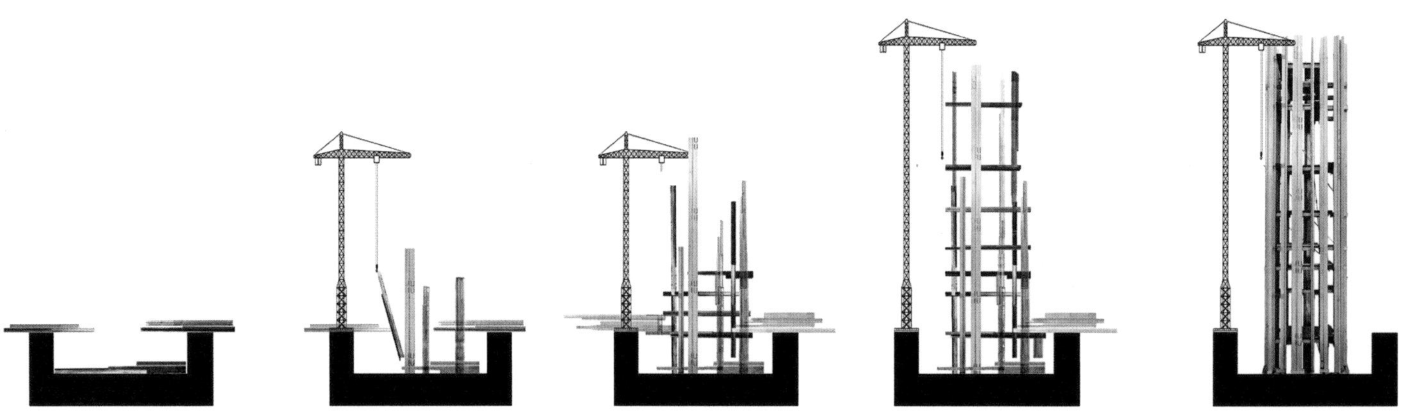

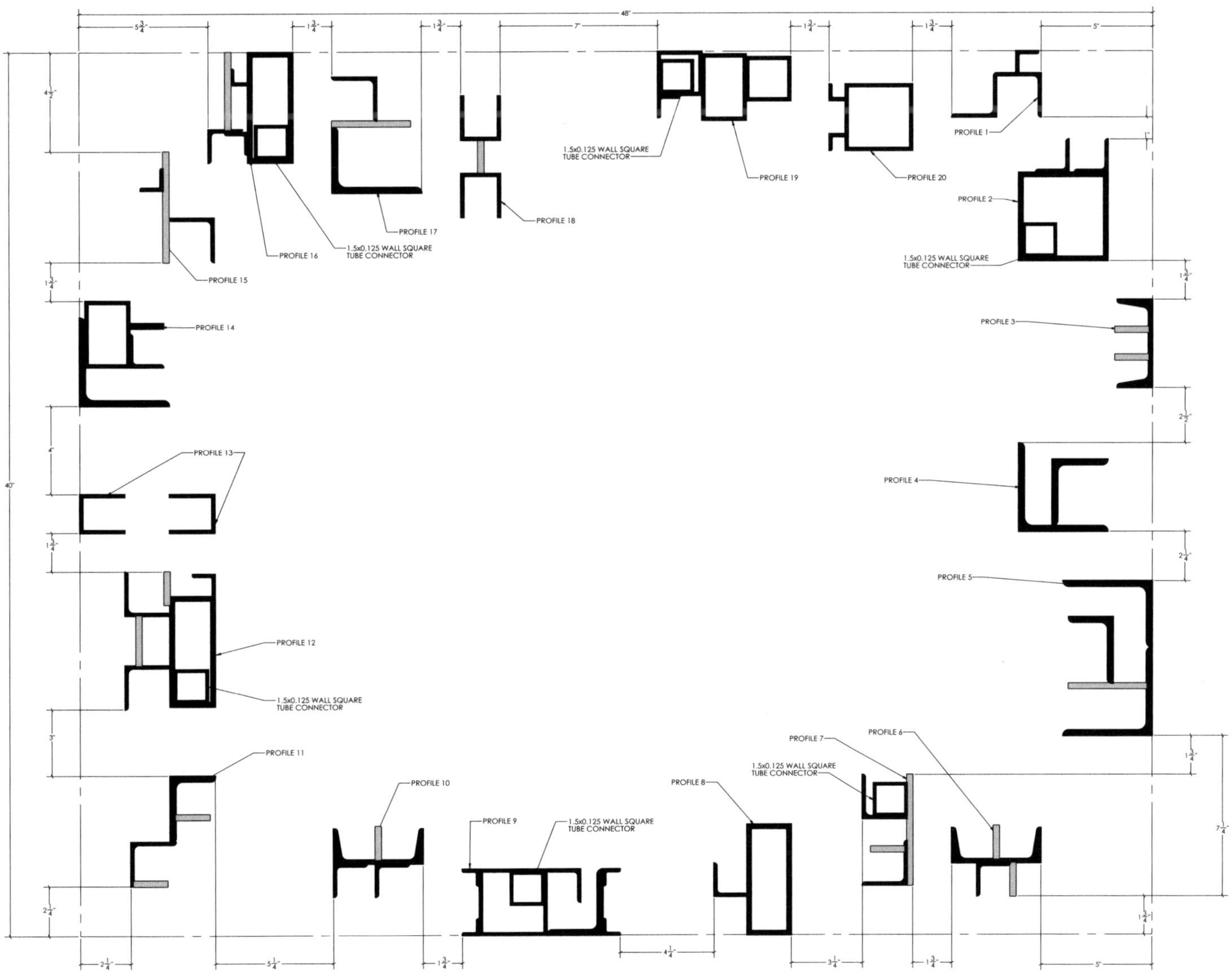

Floorplan. Profiles

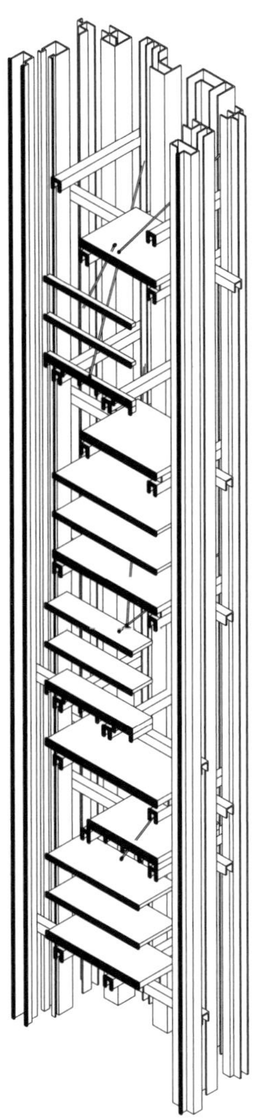

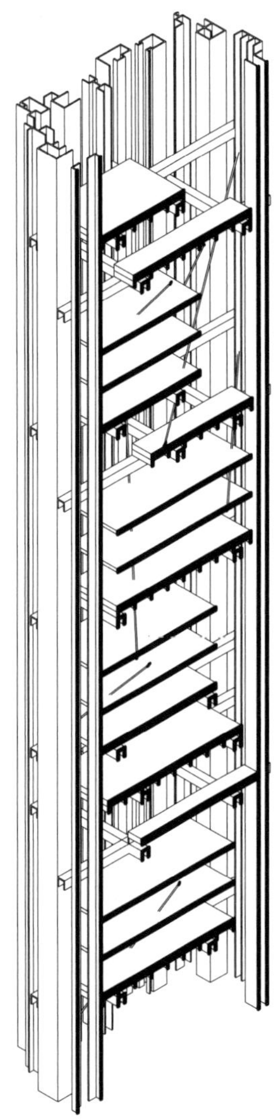

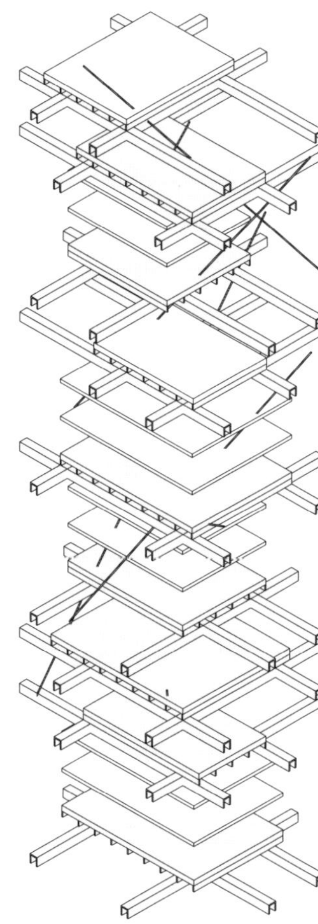

Ensamble Fábrica, Madrid

2016-2019

Architecture emerged from the earth—from the extraction and cultivation of it, and the efforts to move its parts, and from the fascination of then stacking them, putting them together and finally celebrating, discovering and inhabiting the space. The efficiency of the location itself was considered, in terms of the accessibility to matter, reducing thus the effort required. And there was invariably a search for parts that could be put together easily, while tools were designed to work the land, the stones, the fibres and the metals, which, in a way, are also stones. When these instruments became more sophisticated, the places where we could build multiplied, materials and tools could be transported, and new technologies and crafts could be developed. And there was the architect, trying to organise this whole conglomerate. Today, we still have this same mission, but the world and science have changed, as has the way we understand the scale of society and how we distribute the resources we consume.

But we continue to make buildings on the same basis. We transport materials, tools and people to the site where the building is to be erected, and the work is done among everybody, always locally. Works are coordinated outdoors, and materials and small parts are transported daily and continuously so that they can be put together. The building itself is subject to availability, and is conditioned by the local market. All of this means that many of the cutting-edge technologies (i.e. within digital manufacturing, automation and robotics) have still not been introduced into the most redundant and repetitive construction processes. Something that in other industries guarantees quality, efficiency, safety and economy, in construction still appears to be a distant dream.

After years working as architects, builders and, more recently, as manufacturers of our own works, Ensamble Fábrica is the laboratory and manufacturing space that will develop the spaces we dream of, delivering the building parts so that they are ready to be assembled quickly, safely and efficiently in-situ, anywhere in the world. We no longer use a part, a brick, a profile, or conduit that we then transport for its connection on site—instead, we use a "component" of a system, manufactured with today's tools, knowledge and efficiency. And the architect, who in recent times has been reduced to carrying out graphic or decorative labour, here recovers their essential mission of bringing order to an activity as complex and necessary for society as the construction of the physical space. It is an activity necessary for life, so that architecture comes back to the earth.

10t.

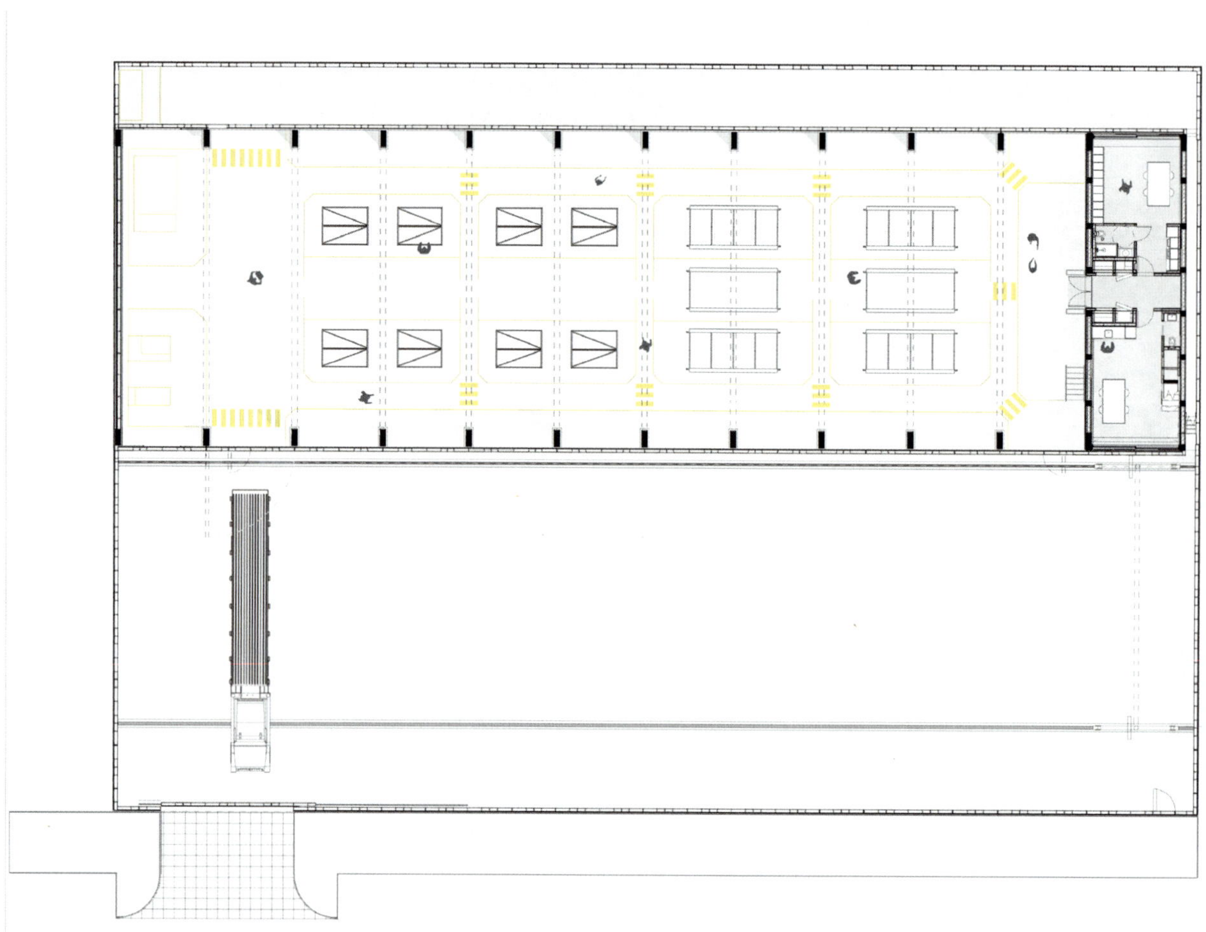

Ground floor

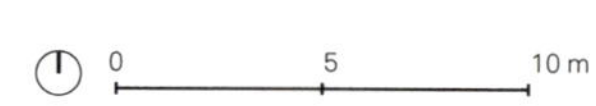

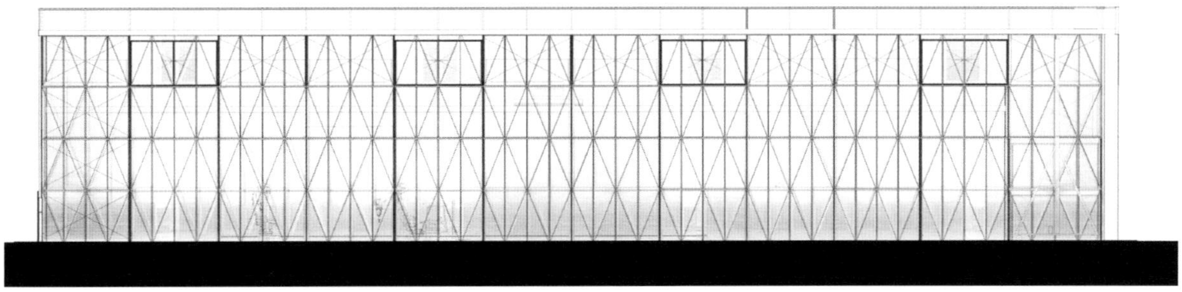

South elevation

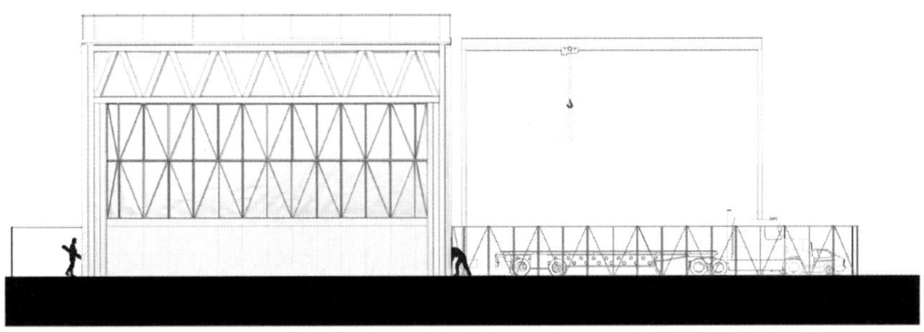

West elevation

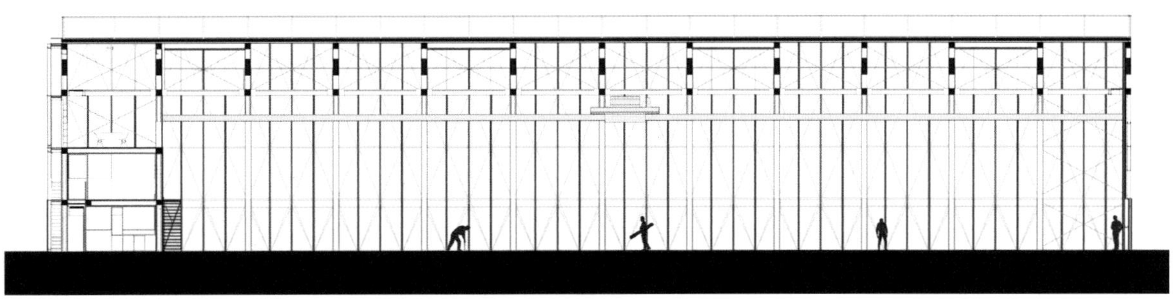

Longitudinal section

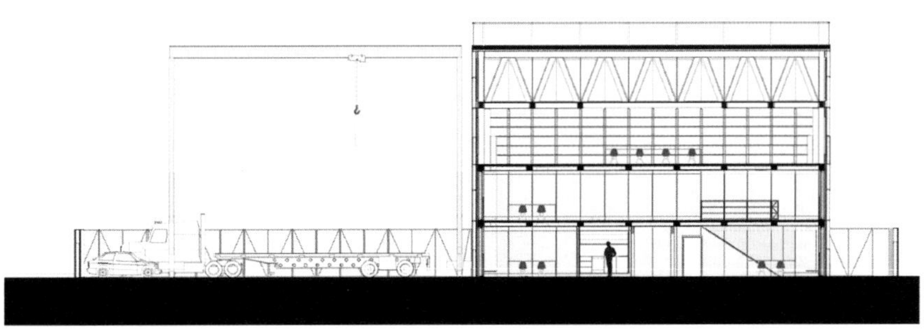

Cross-section

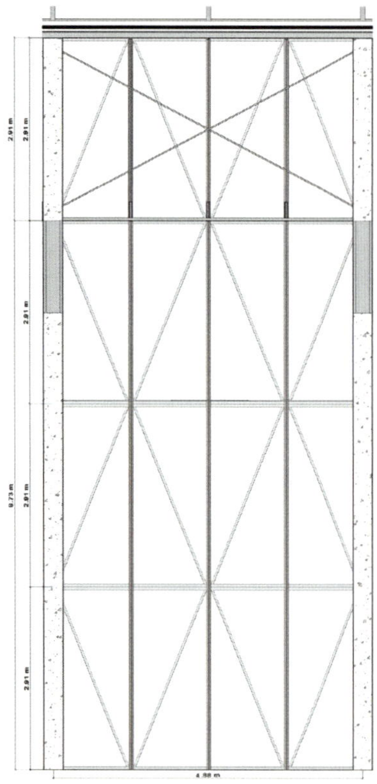
2.91 m
2.91 m
2.91 m
9.73 m
2.91 m
2.91 m
4.38 m

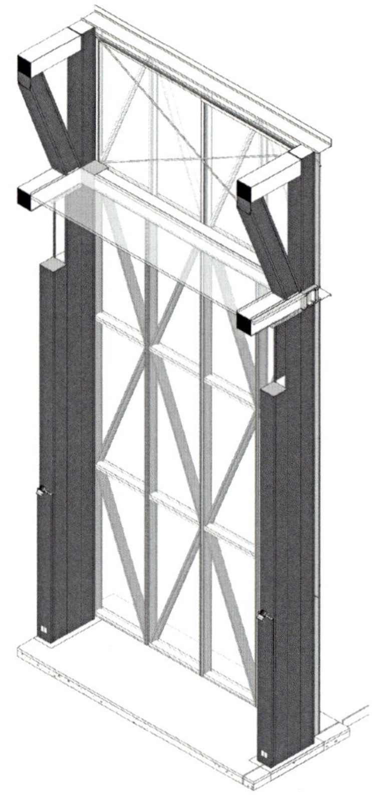

Start-up Centre, Seoul

2017

Our project for a Start-up Centre in Seoul is located in the Changdong-Sanggye area, north of Seoul City, and it forms part of the urban regeneration plan that aims to transform this region into a new economic and cultural hub. An international design competition was launched in 2017 to develop the first building for this area: a centre to support innovation and start-ups, open to multigenerational entrepreneurs, and offering a mixed-use programme including educational, office, residential and public spaces.

Our project is based on an understanding of the infrastructural nature of the site and the wide range of uses to be accommodated under the same roof, in order to build a platform for living, working and learning. The proposed architecture defines a framework that supports and serves the multiple programmes, enabling adequate continuities and discontinuities while still providing a unitary structure. The even distribution of vertical cores throughout the plan contributes to this effort by giving independent access to different zones. This also helps build a primary structure that can support a variety of programmes and architectures over time.

Integrated with the surrounding landscape and infrastructural systems, the building encourages strong connections between the surroundings and the interior activity, creating synergies. Originating from a carved ground, it builds an abstract topography as a transition from the street. The lower levels accommodate the kind of functions that benefit from greater continuity with the adjacent landscape and transportation networks, so that they can be easily accessed by the general public: the car park, the lobby, the gallery, the event space and the café. From the carved ground and through a carefully studied map of vertical circulations, users access the Start-up Centre, the 50 Plus Campus, the NPO Centre and the residential area, each of which have their own particular position in the building. The top levels are reserved for more restricted gatherings, events and terrace spaces—shared by the main users of the building—all with panoramic views. Special attention is paid to circulation and views between different functional areas, with the background context striking a balance between visibility and privacy.

This project strategically selects the resources needed for its construction, and it proposes the use of technologies that will optimise quality, time and therefore construction costs. The primary structure is designed as a hybrid concrete-steel skeleton that can be efficiently assembled, and it integrates the mechanical and transportation systems necessary for the smooth operation of the building. The secondary structures attached to it are for programmes, providing them with particular climatic and light conditions. The materials used to build these spaces adapt to their requirements for permanence, flexibility and expressiveness. The way that the interior architectures and spaces can be redefined, and how the new technologies and services can be progressively incorporated, is all meant to contribute to the resiliency of the complex and its potential to innovate.

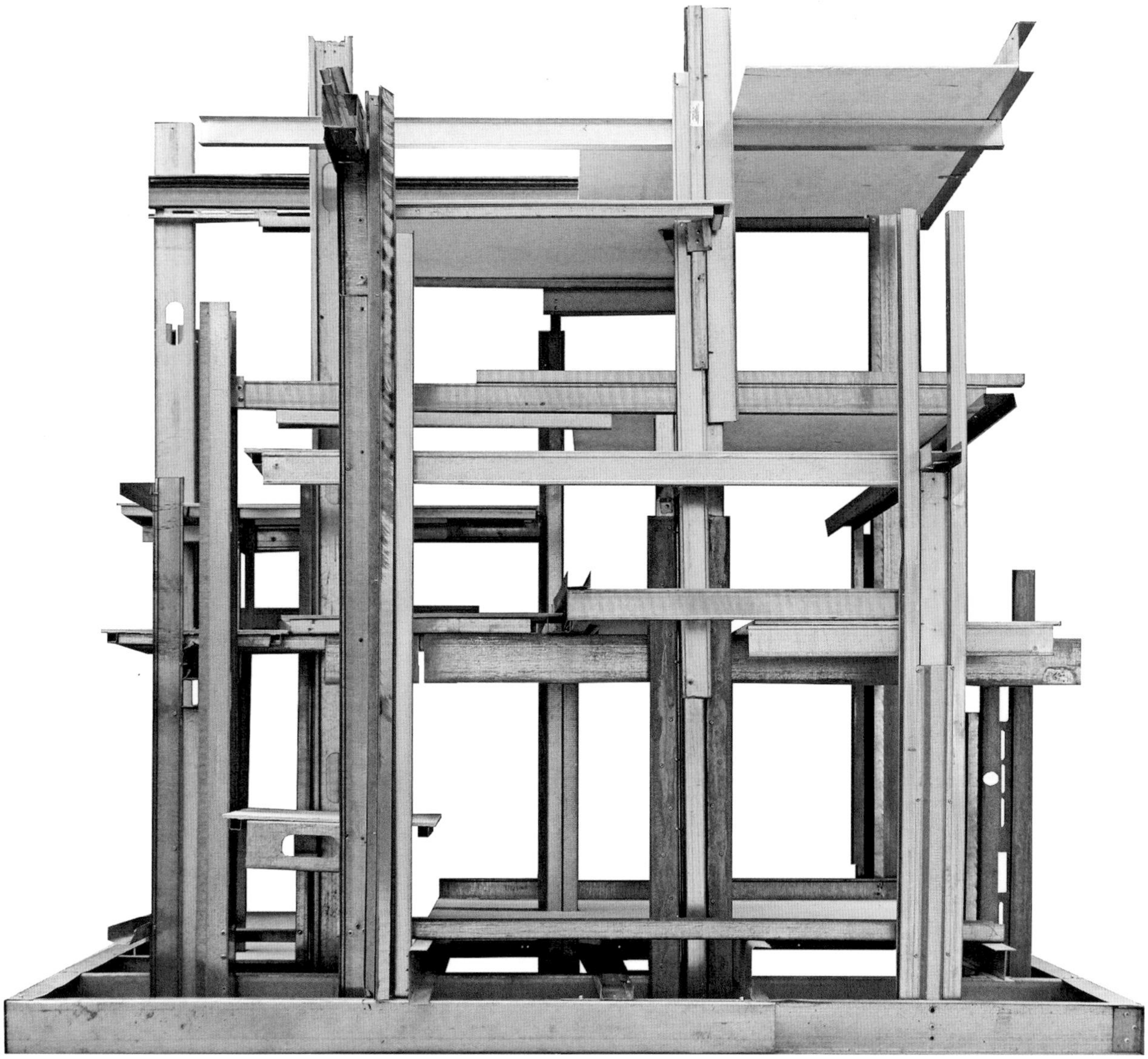

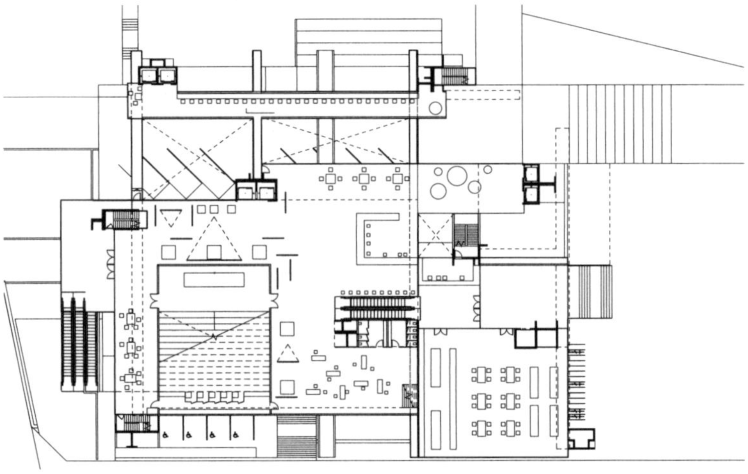

Ground floor

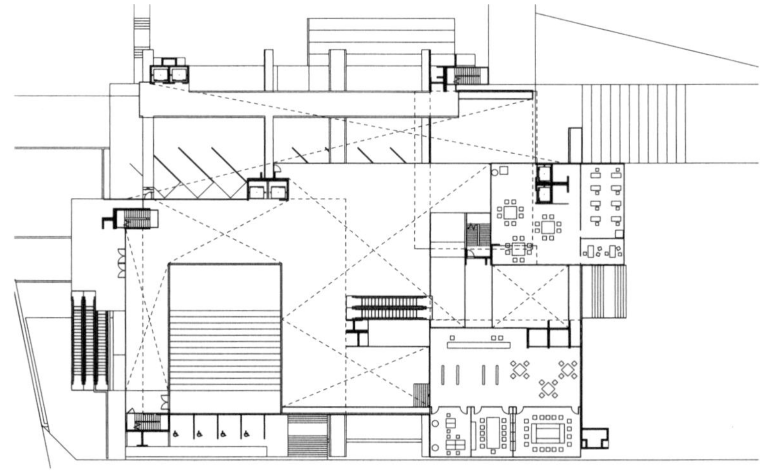

First floor

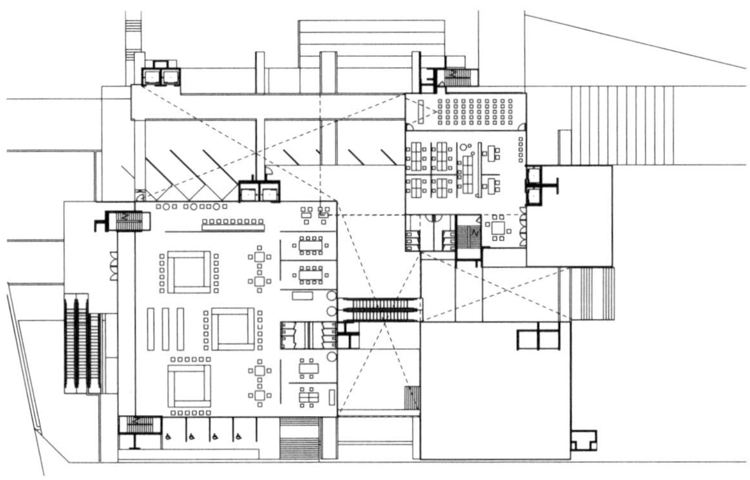

Third floor

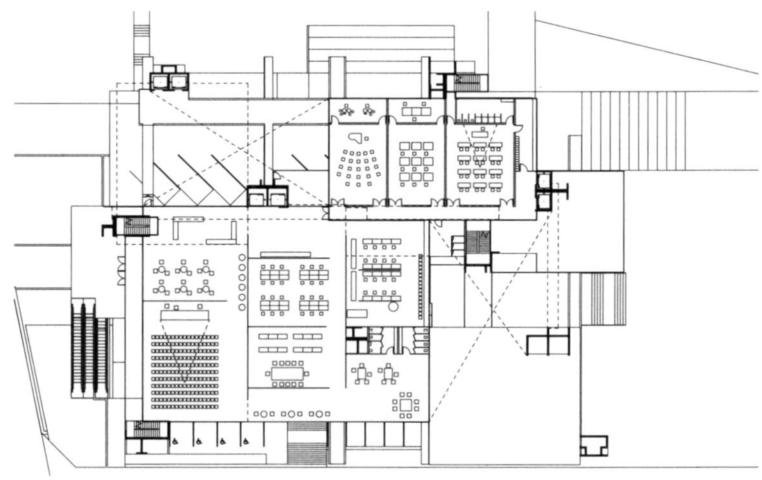

Fourth floor

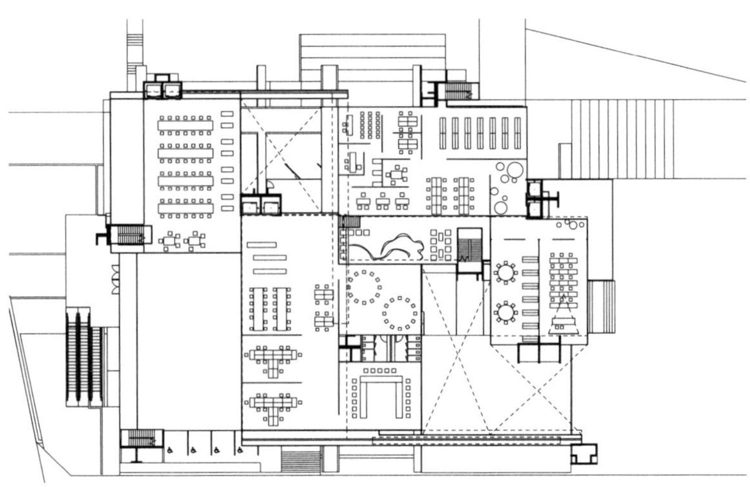

Fifth floor

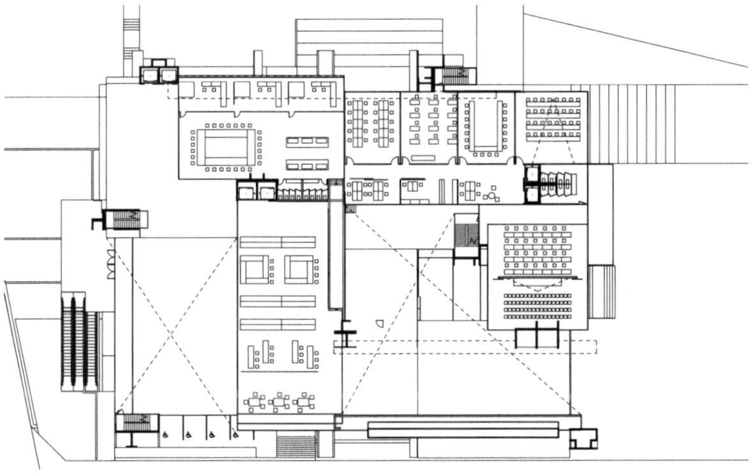

Sixth floor

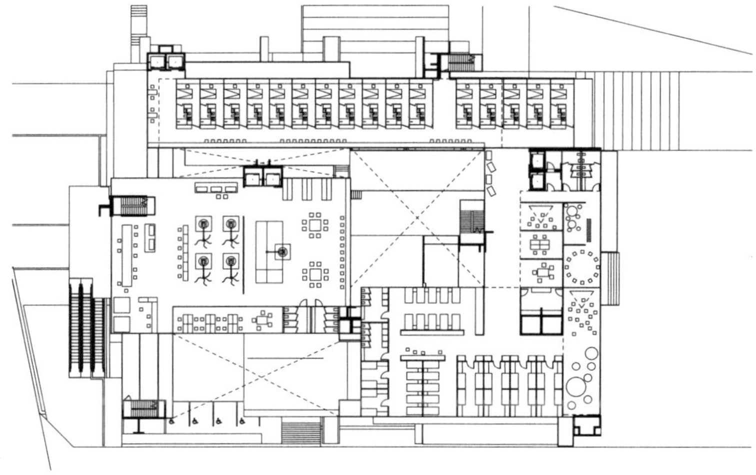

Seventh floor

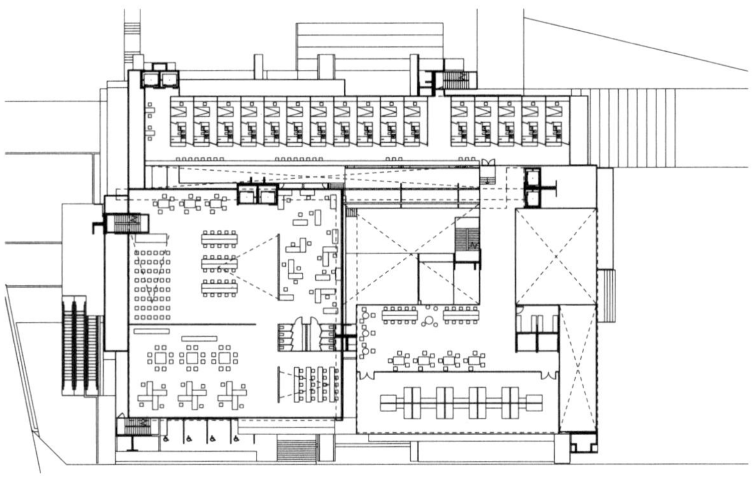

Eighth floor

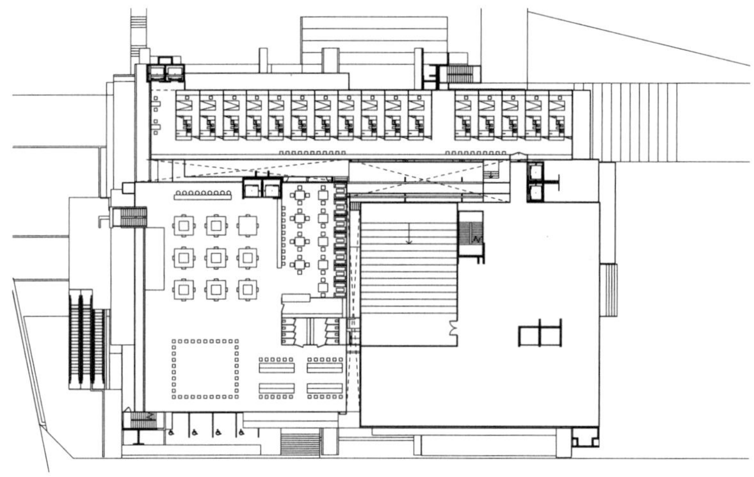

Ninth floor

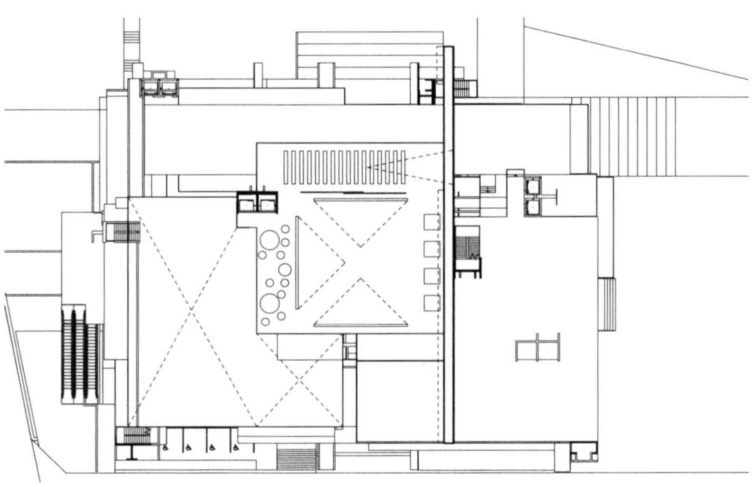

Tenth floor

Cross-section

Cross-section

Reticula, New York

2017

Reticula is a grid, but one that sits atop a rolling land, and it does not have the same grid-like impulse to efficiently connect or divide or arrange. As a metaphor for the urban grid (that so clearly organises most cities today, and is certainly the leitmotif of New York), its design departs from the orthogonal intersection of lines that define and delimit the quadrants in between. Instead, it deforms this instrument of urban planning, so that instead of ordering, it adapts: it adapts to the topography of the land, it adapts to spaces that want to be destinations rather than thoroughfares, and it adapts to the character of the wider context in which it sits. This project deforms, and while doing so, it subverts the idea of the grid, so that quadrants are no longer plots of land, but voids, filled with air and views.

Reticula lies on Governors Island Park, a very special site just south of Manhattan. It is a piece of landscape with outstanding environmental qualities, and it can be reached by ferry from both Manhattan and Brooklyn's closest shores. The island itself, which contains a number of historic buildings in the process of being restored, has also become home to exciting landscape interventions that seek to preserve and enhance the unique characteristics of the site, while also guiding its development. In this evolving ecosystem, Reticula is proposed as a continuation of the recently completed park, enhancing its topography, finding a balanced position in between the hills, lawns, trees, paths, and water, and expanding the island's existing cultural, artistic and recreational functions through a new sheltering structure. Visitors thus participate in a holistic experience of the island, smoothly transitioning from the meandering paths of the park to the covered outdoor spaces of Reticula, and then to its interior, to the ground-roof that offers panoramic views of Governors Island, Manhattan, Brooklyn, Staten Island and New Jersey. Here, landscape is not consumed by the presence of architecture, but rather multiplied by it.

As if extracted from the island's bedrock, Reticula brings together architecture and nature in a way that resounds with the geology of the site. Granite rocks from the island's old seawall, that were used to build the park, are here used again to bring together the cyclopean concrete that will support Reticula's spaces, following patterns and laws that sometimes veer towards what we understand as natural, and other times as architectural. This intriguing ambiguity pushes users to actively explore and interpret, to invent and enjoy.

As part of our research into landscape intervention, this project offers a new opportunity to mediate between urbanisation and habitation, something which is particularly crucial in a city with the density of New York. Furthermore, it suggests the possibility of transcending preconceived ideas about architecture, and also blurring the typological norms so as to allow for renewed thinking about the construction of places.

East elevation

South elevation

Calderona House, Talarrubias

2018-2019

Contemplating nature requires extracting information and processing it with sensibility. This information is often perceived visually, but it can also be heard, breathed in, and, most importantly, felt and embedded into our memory. The emotions that we remember after visiting a space, a place, a landscape, give shape to what Le Corbusier called the "spirit of the place". Transforming this transcendent experience of memory into architecture entails the demanding process of translating abstract concepts into data, such as drawings, photographs, words or models. And this journey, from matter to data, allows us to preserve and enrich memory. As architects, we allow the impulses of our memory to activate the creative subconscious and stimulate our desire to create, build, and interact with a place, with its matter, with its spirit.

Visiting the Calderona estate, in the heart of Extremadura, a place surrounded by hills, marshes, natural exuberance, silence, we come across natural stone eruptions and provocative accidents of material beauty. We also discover forms left there by previous residents that later became vacant, ruined by time, suggestive, opposing the logic of the practical, and embodying the beauty of the natural.

The starting point for our proposal is the intention to revive the accumulated popular knowledge that lies within the masonry stones of the found settlement, and to expose the new domestic spaces to the landscape, via this platform of contemplation, respecting the memory of the place. And upon the stones of Calderona we build other stones, and we free them from any architectural predetermination, so that they can adapt to the orography, both materially and formally. New spaces appear as a result, shaded areas, sheltered rooms, framed views, and so on. We deliberately appropriate existing remains and add to them the intuitive structures within our sensorial memory, the ones that were induced after contemplating and interpreting the data of the landscape, of its matter, of its space, of the spirit of the place.

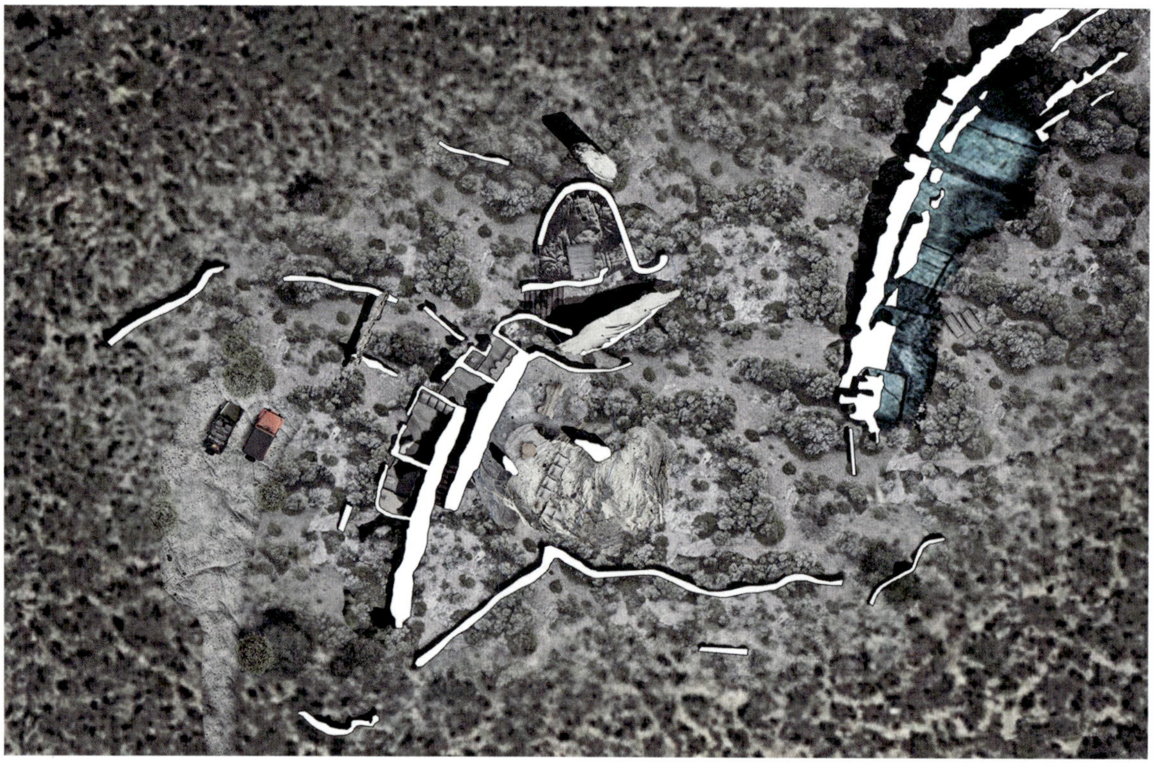

Ground floor

Petrified River, New York

2018-2019

Petrified River is a site-specific installation that occupied Cooper Hewitt Design Museum's garden during the 2019 Design Triennial exhibition entitled *Nature*. It forms part of a research project that explores hybrid typologies, merging the landscape with infrastructure attributes (in order to produce infrastructural works that become extensions of the landscape) or forming artificial landscapes which act as infrastructures. In order to materialise this investigation in a museum context, in New York, and right across from Central Park, we look at the history of the city. Manhattan's transformation process, from wild nature to urbanised, flattened land, has involved enormous efforts and massive exploitation of the terrain—digging, levelling, exploiting, reclaiming, filling—and the resulting disappearance of some of its original geographical features.

This proposal, which consists of a hill, a river and a pond—made of concrete—serves as a petrified metaphor for the rich landscape that Manhattan once was, when it was still known as Mannahatta or the "island of many hills". It aims to embody the intriguing collision between the infrastructural, the industrial, the artistic, the geological... that tricky balance between the artificial and the natural.

The installation was on display from 10th May to 22nd September 2019, after which it travelled to Tippet Rise Art Center, in Montana, to become part of its permanent collection.

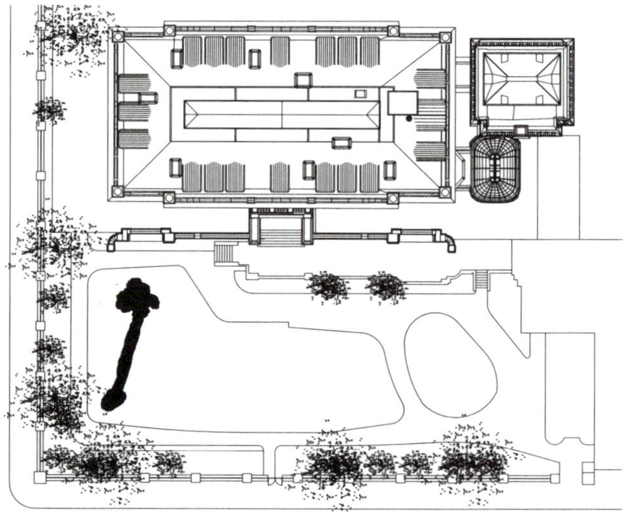

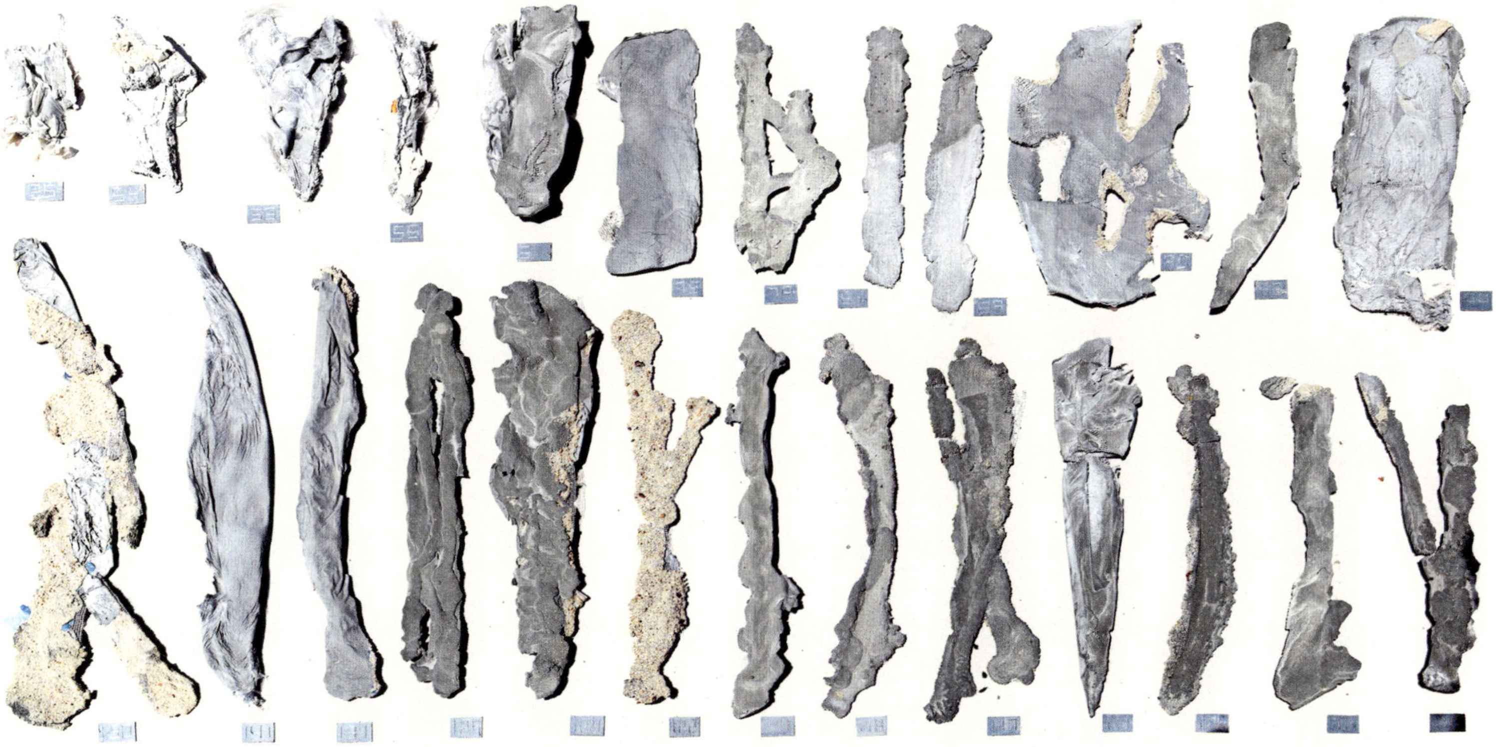

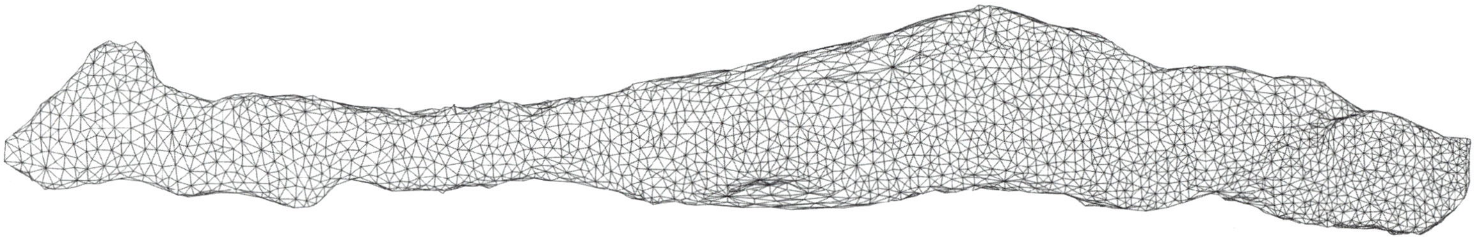

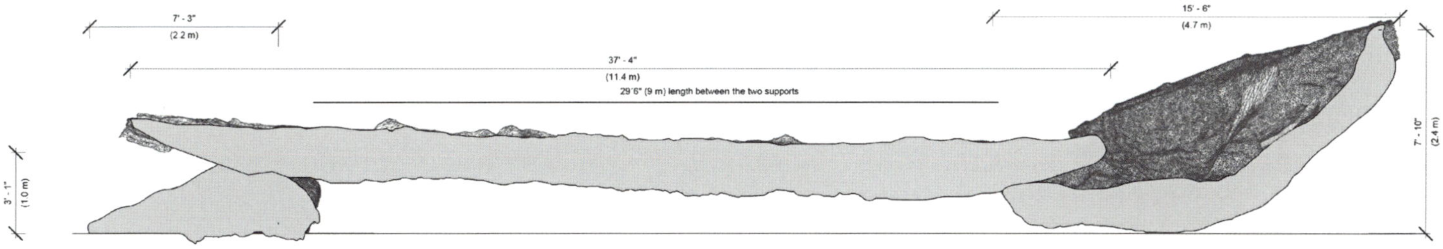
7' - 3"
(2.2 m)
15' - 6"
(4.7 m)
37' - 4"
(11.4 m)
29'6" (9 m) length between the two supports
3' - 1"
(1.0 m)
7' - 10"
(2.4 m)

Ca'n Terra, Menorca

2018-2020

Ca'n Terra is the house of the earth. The fruit that nature gives to us, in the form of a found space, requires tillage and cultivation to imbue this offering with domesticity. If the history of civilisation has evolved by transforming ideas into built work, in Ca'n Terra, the process is inverted, and history is interpreted so that it transforms into architecture. The transfer from a drawing to a built mass is replaced by the translation from given matter to digital data, by means of the architectural reading of a geological discovery.

The discovered space has industrial logic, as a former Marès stone quarry; it has artistic potential, as a sublime cavern carved by hand; and it has a mineral nature, as an extract from the stony landscape on the island of Menorca. Finding this excavated space in the guts of the earth, and reinventing its use, implies writing a new story that can rescue it from abandonment.

As our first contact, we enter the space like explorers would, equipped with the technology that expands our vision in the dark. We cast millions of laser dots onto the wrinkles of the continuous stone surface, and we register, with millimetric precision, the solid structure that was already built for us and is now ready to be polished and inhabited. Following this scan, the architect's eye directs, interprets, and creates the space again. That's why the discovery is considered a new work, destined this time to become a room for contemplating nature. In lieu of an imposing action, the kind that architecture often exerts on the environment, we propose a trip deep into the interior being of matter, and we recognise the freedom with which it gives us spaces to live.

The Tent, Costa da Morte

2020

The Tent covers the space like a blanket. Its geometries adapt to the airy body that it delimits and embraces, without constraining it. Air and light flow through its openings, and the landscape sneaks in too, filling the cracks in the material.

This architecture is hand-moulded, with hands that fold, connect, dream up the structure and the space, in unison. Starting with the model, which serves as a sketch and a miniature construction, we go on to data, scanning each movement and each detail, guided by intuition. After the designing comes the engineering, and then back to the designing. All of this happens over just five days, and then another five days to carry out the action in the rural destination. The construction is reminiscent of the design process in terms of its dynamic; the form has already been established, the structures calculated, the lines marked out. The work gets underway by drawing the reinforcing bars in three dimensions; checking the measurements, proportions and orientations on site. And when the strokes have been validated, we start painting the structure, as if we were painting over a sketched-out canvas, adding material, texture and colour in one unique, unrepeatable gesture. Layer by layer, its flexible folds get more rigid, its elastic membranes harden, its damp skin dries out. Layer by layer, an architecture materialises, one which is both fabric-like and rock-like, light and permanent, fluid and stony. Either one or the other, depending on how you look at it, or how you touch it. It rises from the ground and it leans gently, as if it were meant to be a short-term structure, but its supports have taken root and they hold up a space that lies between the trees, looking out at the sea. It silently hopes to be taken in by nature, embraced, welcomed into the fold.

The Tent, Costa da Morte

Credits

Hemeroscopium House

Location Las Rozas (Madrid), Spain
Architect Antón García-Abril
Project team Javier Cuesta (building engineer), Débora Mesa (associate architect), Elena Pérez (project manager), Marina Otero, Ricardo Sanz, Jorge Consuegra
Design and construction years 2005-2008
Developer Hemeroscopium
Construction company Materia Inorgánica
Consultants Obradoiro Enxeñeiros (MEP), Jesús Huerga (structure)
Surface 400 m²
Photographs Iwan Baan

The Truffle

Location Costa da Morte (A Coruña), Spain
Architect Antón García-Abril
Project team Javier Cuesta (building engineer), Débora Mesa (associate architect), Ricardo Sanz (project manager)
Design and construction years 2006-2010
Developer Ensamble Studio
Consultants Obradoiro Enxeñeiros (MEP), Jesús Huerga (structure)
Collaborating companies Galicorte (concrete cut), Macías Derribos (excavation), Suministros Zúrich (seafood), Ganadería Paulina (cow), Francheteau (audiovisual production)
Surface 25 m²
Photographs Ensamble Studio, Iwan Baan

Reader's House

Location Matadero, Madrid, Spain
Architects Ensamble Studio (Antón García-Abril & Débora Mesa)
Project team Javier Cuesta (building engineer), Marina Otero (project manager), Elena Pérez, Ricardo Sanz, Alba Cortés
Design and construction years 2006-2012
Developer Fundación Germán Sánchez Ruipérez
Consultants Úrculo Engineering (MEP), Jesús Huerga (structure)
Collaborating company Prainsa (prestressed concrete)
Surface 7,500 m²
Photographs Roland Halbe

Telcel Theatre

Location Mexico City, Mexico
Architects Antón García-Abril
Project team Javier Cuesta (building engineer), Débora Mesa (associate architect), Elena Pérez (associate architect), Alba Cortés (project manager), Joaquín Gallegos, Alba Beroiz, Jaime Alcayde, Cristina Moya, Juan Ruiz Antón, Tomaso Boano, Federico Letizia
Design and construction years 2007-2012
Developer SGAE – Grupo Carso
Project management INPROS
General contractor Grupo PC
Consultant Colinas de Buen (structure)
Surface 11,500 m²
Photographs Iwan Baan

Cyclopean House

Location Boston (Massachusetts), USA
Architects Ensamble Studio (Antón García-Abril & Débora Mesa)
Project team Javier Cuesta (building engineer), Ricardo Sanz (project manager), Borja Soriano, Massimo Loia, Walter Cuccuru, Valentina Giacomini, Marietta Spyrou, Juanjo Fernández, Federica Zunino, Marian Stanislav, Chung-Wen Wu, Yannis Karababas
Design and construction years 2014-2015
Developer Ensamble Studio
Construction Company Materia Inorgánica
Consultants Úrculo Engineering (MEP), Jesús Huerga (structure)
Surface 240 m²
Photographs Iwan Baan

Structures of Landscape

Location Fishtail (Montana), USA
Architects Ensamble Studio (Antón García-Abril & Débora Mesa)
Project team Javier Cuesta (building engineer), Ricardo Sanz (project manager), Massimo Loia, Simone Cavallo, Borja Soriano, Giorgia Pisano, Walter Cuccuru, Marcos Jiménez, Laura Puzzoni
Design and construction years 2014-2016
Developer Tippet Rise (Cathy & Peter Halstead), Sidney E. Frank Foundation
Construction management OSM
Consultant Jesús Huerga (structure)
Collaborating companies Davis and Sons (concrete), CMG (excavations), Mountain West Steel (reinforcements)
Surface 4,600 hectares (masterplan), 600 m² (structures)
Photographs Ensamble Studio, Iwan Baan

Zig Zag House

Location San Martín de Valdeiglesias (Madrid), Spain
Architects Ensamble Studio (Antón García-Abril & Débora Mesa)
Project team Javier Cuesta, Ricardo Sanz, Simone Cavallo, Massimo Loia, Borja Soriano
Design and construction year 2020
Consultants Úrculo Engineering (MEP), Jesús Huerga (structure)
Surface 700 m² (total), 320 m² (interior)
Photographs Ensamble Studio

Towers of Landscape

Architects Ensamble Studio (Antón García-Abril & Débora Mesa)
Project team Javier Cuesta, Borja Soriano, Álvaro Catalán, Michele Matteo Marcotulli, Massimo Loia, Areej Alchalabi, Mónica Acosta
Design and construction years 2016-2017
Photographs Ensamble Studio

Big Bang Tower

Location Chicago, USA
Architects Ensamble Studio (Antón García-Abril & Débora Mesa)
Project team Javier Cuesta, Borja Soriano, Simone Cavallo, Massimo Loia, Silvia Sáez, Joakim Aslund
Design and construction years 2016-2017
Structural consultant Torroja Engineering
Photographs Ensamble Studio

Ensamble Fábrica

Location Pinto (Madrid), Spain
Architects Ensamble Studio (Antón García-Abril & Débora Mesa)
Project team Javier Cuesta (building engineer), Borja Soriano, Niccolò Ciaccheri, Federico Lepre, Massimo Loia, Álvaro Catalán, Mengyuan Cao, María José Carrillo, Mónica Acosta, Elyse Khoury, Marco Antrodicchia, Arianna Sebastiani
Design and construction years 2016-2019
Developer Ensamble Studio/WoHo Systems
Construction management Materia Inorgánica
Consultants Úrculo Engineering (MEP), Jesús Huerga (structure)
Surface 1,150 m²
Photographs Iwan Baan

Start-up Centre

Location Changdong-Sanggye, Seoul, South Korea
Architects Ensamble Studio (Antón García-Abril & Débora Mesa)
Project team Simone Cavallo, Massimo Loia, Joakim Aslund, Argyris Mavronikolas, Mengyuan Cao, Mónica Acosta
Design and construction year 2017
Developer City of Seoul
Surface 334,750 m² (masterplan), 16,500 m² (building)
Photographs Ensamble Studio

Reticula

Location Governors Island (New York), USA
Architects Ensamble Studio (Antón García-Abril & Débora Mesa)
Project team Javier Cuesta, Simone Cavallo, Massimo Loia, Marcos Jiménez
Design and construction year 2017
Surface 27,220 m² (footprint area), 54,440 m² (total floor area)
Photographs Ensamble Studio

Calderona House

Location Talarrubias (Badajoz), Spain
Architects Ensamble Studio (Antón García-Abril & Débora Mesa)
Project team Javier Cuesta, Massimo Loia, Mengyuan Cao, Álvaro Catalán
Design and construction years 2018-2019
Surface 100,750 m² (site area), 700 m² (total floor area)
Photographs Ensamble Studio

Petrified River

Location New York, USA
Architects Ensamble Studio (Antón García-Abril & Débora Mesa)
Project team Javier Cuesta (building engineer), Borja Soriano (project manager), Massimo Loia, Mengyuan Cao, Álvaro Catalán, Mónica Acosta, Niccolò Ciaccheri, Federico Lepre, Marco Antrodicchia, Arianna Sebastianni, Sebastián Zapata, Riccardo Gialloreto, Pinjung Chen, Yun Tso Chung
Design and construction years 2018-2019
Client Cooper Hewitt Smithsonian Design Museum (New York), CUBE Design Museum (The Netherlands)
Sponsor Sidney E. Frank Foundation (Tippet Rise Fund)
Structural consultant Torroja Ingeniería (José M. Simón-Talero and Alberto Fernández)
Photographs James Florio

Ca'n Terra

Location Menorca (Balearic Islands), Spain
Architects Ensamble Studio (Antón García-Abril & Débora Mesa)
Project team Javier Cuesta (building engineer), Borja Soriano (project manager), Claudia Armas, Álvaro Catalán, Massimo Loia, Marco Antrodicchia, Sebastián Zapata, Arianna Sebastiani, Ekam Sahni, Yu-Ting Li, Joel Kim, Gonzalo Peña, Yvonne Asiimwe, Mónica Acosta
Design and construction years 2018-2020
Developer Ensamble Studio
Construction management Ensamble Studio
Consultant Úrculo Engineering (MEP)
Surface 1,000 m²
Photographs Iwan Baan

The Tent

Location Costa da Morte (A Coruña), Spain
Architects Ensamble Studio (Antón García-Abril & Débora Mesa)
Project team Javier Cuesta (building engineer), Borja Soriano, Álvaro Catalán, Fernando González
Design and construction year 2020
Developer Ensamble Studio
Construction management Materia Inorgánica
Consultant Jesús Huerga (Structure)
Surface 35 m2
Photographs Iwan Baan

NEXUS

Modus Operandi

Antón García-Abril, Débora Mesa

Modus Operandi

Antón García-Abril, Débora Mesa

The particular circumstances around a given building's development and realisation, as well as the circumstances of time, throughout the whole protracted process, always take place amid the frenzy of the present. And yet, generally speaking, the present is out of our control.

However, one thing we can control is the future, so, in the frantic here and now, we try to combine the power of our creative urges with the specific ideas we bring to the table. As such, the future is all that matters; we are able to manipulate it. With these brief words, we want to talk about our future, and the methodologies and spaces that so boldly lead the way; we want to describe it, order it, express it and then ideally have the guile, the skill and the luck to ensure that the present and its circumstances can handle such a plan. In terms of the future of our own practice, we have unspeakable ambitions that aim to take architecture to a new level, to create new languages and find a possible communion between human beings, their space and their time.

No clients, no commissions

We have never believed in commissions as a driving force in their own right, and we have devoted most of our lives to inventing future-looking projects with all the hope, aspiration (and patience) that one day they might find their due time and place. We are motivated by the issues that interest us, that disturb us, ones that we consider to be urgent and relevant, and so our creative actions respond to the need to make the kind of architecture that meets today's demands, with as few restrictions as possible. We have never needed a client to tell us exactly what to do, nor have we required a predefined programme to give us focus, and our rhythm is never set by any external timer. Even so, we have of course had clients, excellent ones, but the relationship has hardly ever been as stated in the professional contract; generally, when such a relationship has endured, it has transcended the predetermined roles, and alliances have been forged in which aims, risks and discoveries have been shared between us all. We have often decided to be our own clients, self-commissioning works that have proven to be fundamental for us in terms of finding and positioning ourselves as architects, in order to define the kind of architecture we believe in, and to let the work do the talking. We trust that our steadfastness will magnetically draw in clients, programmes and resources that somehow match our vision. We firmly believe in the visionary architect, one who is ahead of their time, and who takes on the responsibility entailed within all acts of creation. Since we do not depend on commissions, we have been able to pick and choose, and so we feel completely in control of who we are and what we do. Thus, architecture is our lifeblood, it is what connects each and every one of our days, and our approach to it lets us to look to our professional and personal future knowing that its foundations rest upon our own experience.

The driving forces

After twenty years in the field of architecture, a handful of buildings and a great deal of observation about the variables in the market, in technology, in urban and civic development, we now see how our work has been paving an endless path, slowly but surely, one which still guides our upcoming work.

This path started with our first steps, our early lived experiences, our impressions of working in the granite quarries in Galicia, where, for the first time and very clearly, we saw the direct link between the logic of the industrial processes and the transformation of the landscape: images, sounds and energies made a mark on our conscience and subconscious. This subconscious is perhaps the reason why our most recent project rediscovers this link, once more in a quarry, albeit an abandoned, sandstone one this time, in the middle of the Mediterranean Sea.

A multitude of projects in-between—be they in the form of ideas, prototypes or gladly realised ones—lay down, stone by stone, the paths that join ideas, share experiences and transport visions. These projects are not final destinations, but rather resting points, to take a breather, to make sure that we are on the same page, to plan the next move, to enjoy the road already travelled, to take stock. Some projects look into the industrial, into new opportunities and efficiencies in the processes of material transformation, proposing alternative uses for existing products or creating other products that follow better logics. From the Hemeroscopium House, to the Wo-Ho start-up, the issue of prefabrication has evolved from the re-using of known systems to the creation of alternatives that invite us to rethink the economics, ecology and topology of quality architecture, in a way that responds to the overarching urban and technological challenges.

Some of our other projects learn from geology; they look at the land, searching around its internal rationales to find unexpected, indeterminable, unthinkable architectures. They reinvent the language, relinquishing all dogmas and conventions, while taking advantage of geographical references and artistic liberties. From The Truffle to the Structures of Landscape in Montana, or our work in the Arabian desert, our investigations look to build architectural spaces that become the landscape, that are inserted into the place as an intrinsic part of it—architecture that the land could reclaim as its own.

All of these projects work with material by exploiting its potential, by moulding it in ingenious ways to respond to the laudable mission of constructing spaces for the human being to inhabit, and also by reconnecting the material with the nature from which it is extracted. They all contribute, with a different energy, in pushing us forward in the tireless and ongoing search that leads all of our efforts.

The architecture of action

Working with the material means getting your hands dirty, really getting stuck in. It means thinking whilst doing, so that the material also thinks and talks. Our ability to create, as architects, is in turn amplified by our growing ability to build, as constructors. We shape material in order to describe structures, spaces and textures before having drawn a single line, sometimes even before having thought about what architecture will emerge from the action. By thinking with our hands and heads at the same time, we put our whole body to work, at the service of our creative impulses. The chemical and electrical signals multiply as and when our brain gives the instructions, while it also learns from what the body does, what it sees, what it touches and feels.

The leap from intuition to production is an immediate one, and the randomness of the action is built-in, from the very start, as a defining variable within the project's process. The leap from sketch to prototype comes about following a deeply architectural process which values engineering, building precision and professional skill as its greatest assets. Our starting point is always the reinterpretation or reinvention of a certain part, be it a wall, a beam or a slab, in order to set the rules of the game as part of a plan of action, rather than as part of a blueprint. This plan of action is choreographed and rehearsed, again and again, so that the consequences of this experience determine the main aspects of the materiality, the form and space, but above all so that they suggest how we are to undertake said plan, at scale, and at the location of the project. We never set out on any mission when we already know, beforehand, what the result will be, and we have blind faith in the sessions that we often hold with all the members of the studio, when we come together in chorus. These orchestrated events often turn into a chaotic dance, and sometimes into magic. What we do know is that we are delving into the most profoundly creative part of the human being, that which cannot be expressed in words, and that which is not about muses or Lorca-style angels, but rather one that listens to the desire that lies within the creative core of emotion itself. With no clearly set-out plan, we embrace improvisation, guided by intuition and our accumulated experience. Our work as architects freely gravitates towards that of artists, scientists and engineers of processes, of methods… those who are interested in the links between parts, in actions and reactions, in underlying energies, with no rush to get to a fi-

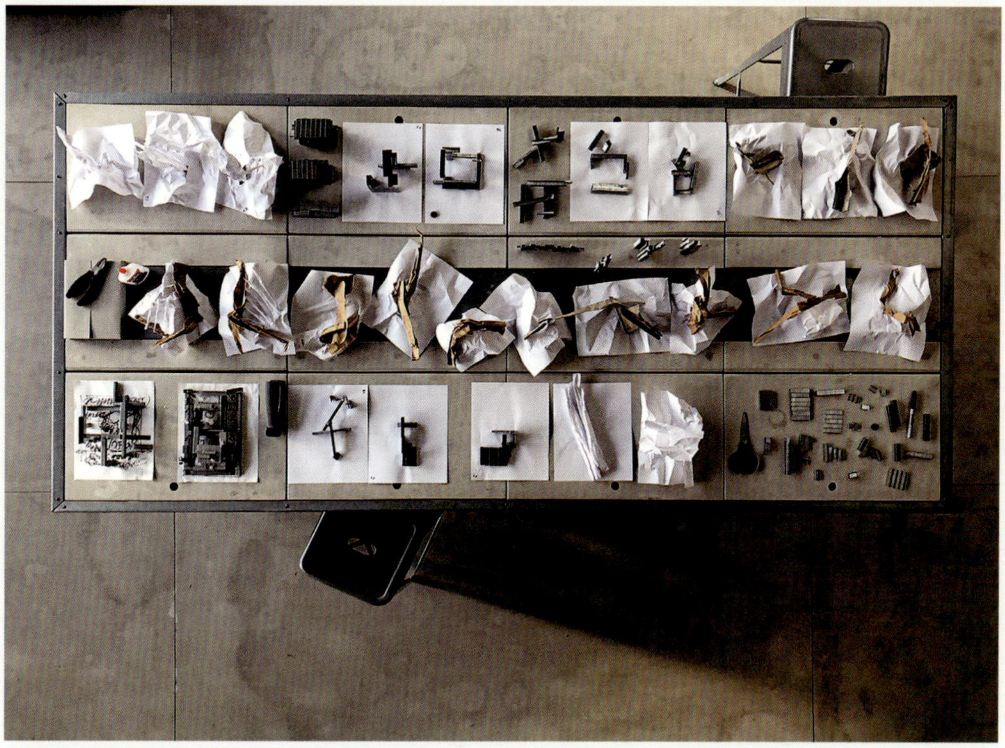

nal result. The key to our design lies in choosing the tools, defining the rules of the game and letting the rest work itself out amid the dance. If we control the process, then, wherever we end up, it will ultimately make sense.

The Workspaces

The fruits of these sessions, which we activate and document meticulously, lie in wait for years, hoping for a new gaze, a timely rescue that gives them meaning and opportunity. And we save these actions as our stock, as part of a living archive that we keep inside our workplaces, which themselves are architectures also built by our hands, inherent parts of our visions and instigators of our missions.

This is why we decided to move these spaces for work and for reference to two very different sites—one of them, a factory in an industrial park on the outskirts of Madrid, and the other an abandoned landscape in Menorca—both of which were designed and conceived so that we could work with our hands, and to let us revert the process that goes from data to matter, which all architecture of action involves. Here, first we do, and afterwards we observe, measure, interpret, digitalise, calculate. Process, action, play. These are the words with which we dismantle the rigidity that architecture uses to deal the rigour of the project.

Here, where the architecture of action discovers its right time, where the moments of creative explosion can neither be pre-empted nor scheduled, we freeze and encase the fruits of our architectural impulses, so that they can rest, and then awaken later on, when the future is ready to receive them.

Biography

Ensamble Studio

© James Florio

Ensamble Studio is an architectural studio founded in 2000. It is led by Antón García-Abril and Débora Mesa, with virtual offices and physical laboratories in Madrid, Menorca and Boston. Their work has been extensively published in both print and digital media, and it has been exhibited worldwide, notably at the Cooper Hewitt Design Triennial in New York (2019), the Chicago Architecture Biennial (2017), the Venice Architecture Biennale (2016 and 2010), The Museum of Modern Art (MoMA), New York (2015), etc. The studio has won several international prizes, such as the 2019 RIBA Charles Jencks Award, the 2017 Architizer A+Award, and the 2016 NCSEA Excellence in Structural Engineering Award, among others.

Antón García-Abril (Madrid, 1969) studied Architecture at the School of Architecture of the Polytechnic University of Madrid (ETSAM-UPM), where he holds a doctorate degree. He was awarded the Spanish Academy Prize in Rome in 1996. He is a registered architect in the US and Europe. Since 2012, García-Abril has been a professor at the School of Architecture and Planning of the Massachusetts Institute of Technology (MIT), Cambridge, where he also co-founded the POPlab (Prototypes of Prefabrication Research Laboratory) that same year.

Débora Mesa (Madrid, 1981) studied Architecture at the School of Architecture of the Polytechnic University of Madrid (ETSAM-UPM), where she holds a Master's degree and also completed her doctorate studies. She is a registered architect in Europe. Since 2018, Mesa has been the Ventulett Chair in Architectural Design at the Georgia Tech School of Architecture, Atlanta. Before this, she served as a research scientist at MIT from 2013 to 2018, where she co-founded the POPlab.

García-Abril and Mesa have progressively redefined the role of the architect, expanding their skills as designers by also becoming developers, contractors, manufacturers and inventors. Their partner Javier Cuesta has been a key member of their team from its foundation, and he has contributed with his engineering background to the consolidation of a hands-on approach to architecture. With Cuesta, Borja Soriano and Israel Ruiz, García-Abril and Mesa co-founded WoHo in 2020, marking a new starting point in their research into offsite technologies.